TRUE TO LIFE

INTERMEDIATE

Ruth Gairns
Stuart Redman

with *Joanne Collie*

CLASS BOOK

CAMBRIDGE
UNIVERSITY PRESS

PUBLISHED BY THE PRESS SYNDICATE OF THE UNIVERSITY OF CAMBRIDGE
The Pitt Building, Trumpington Street, Cambridge, United Kingdom

CAMBRIDGE UNIVERSITY PRESS
The Edinburgh Building, Cambridge CB2 2RU, UK   http://www.cup.cam.ac.uk
40 West 20th Street, New York, NY 10011–4211, USA   http://www.cup.org
10 Stamford Road, Oakleigh, Melbourne 3166, Australia
Ruiz de Alarcón 13, 28014 Madrid, Spain

First published 1996
Seventh printing 2000

Printed in the United Kingdom at the University Press, Cambridge

ISBN 0 521 45632 0 Class Book
ISBN 0 521 45631 2 Personal Study Workbook
ISBN 0 521 45630 4 Teacher's Book
ISBN 0 521 45629 0 Class Cassette Set
ISBN 0 521 45628 2 Personal Study Workbook Cassette
ISBN 0 521 48576 2 Personal Study Workbook Audio CD

CONTENTS

COURSE OVERVIEW ... 4

1 LOOKING BACK AND LOOKING FORWARD ... 6
2 HOW DOES THAT SOUND? ... 13
3 GAMES PEOPLE PLAY ... 19
4 NEWSPAPERS AND MAGAZINES ... 26
5 RELATIONSHIPS ... 34
6 LIFE'S LITTLE CHORES ... 40
7 COURSES ... 47
8 ALL IN A DAY'S WORK ... 54
9 FROM THE CRADLE TO THE GRAVE ... 60
10 PHONAHOLICS ... 67
11 GOODS AND SERVICES ... 74
12 BARE NECESSITIES ... 80
13 WHO IS REALLY ON TRIAL? ... 86
14 TALL STORIES, SHORT STORIES ... 93
15 LOVE THY NEIGHBOUR ... 100
16 YES AND NO ... 107
17 PACKAGING ... 114
18 HONESTLY SPEAKING ... 121
19 PLAIN ENGLISH ... 129
20 ART AND SOCIETY ... 136
21 DARE YOURSELF TO SUCCEED ... 143
22 FORCES OF NATURE ... 150

GRAMMAR REFERENCE ... 158
ADDITIONAL MATERIAL ... 171
TAPESCRIPTS ... 174
IRREGULAR VERBS ... 175
ACKNOWLEDGEMENTS ... 176

COURSE OVERVIEW

Unit	Language focus	Vocabulary	Topics	Review
1 LOOKING BACK AND LOOKING FORWARD	past simple revision *will* for prediction different uses of present continuous	adjectives describing emotion learning	personal memories how the world is changing methods of revision	
2 HOW DOES THAT SOUND?	comparative structures countable/uncountable nouns	ways of talking adjectives class words, e.g. *toys, furniture*	how to improve your pronunciation comparing voices types of noise	Unit 1
3 GAMES PEOPLE PLAY	likes and dislikes preferences and opinions verb + *-ing* form or infinitive preposition + *-ing* form	sport and leisure verb and adjective + preposition ways of paraphrasing	giving opinions about different sports game shows on TV leisure activities	Unit 1 Unit 2
4 NEWSPAPERS AND MAGAZINES	past simple and present perfect *for, since* and *yet*	newspapers adjectives describing people	social issues magazine survey choosing the best stories for a magazine newspapers in different countries	Unit 2 Unit 3
5 RELATIONSHIPS	revision of question forms use of possessive *'s* probability and possibility prepositions in *wh-* questions	relationships verb + prepositions	is a first child different from other children? who do you trust the most? famous family tree	Unit 3 Unit 4
6 LIFE'S LITTLE CHORES	past continuous reflexive pronouns *get* + past participle functional language	phrasal verbs verb prefix *un-* accidents and injuries	household chores a history of queuing cross-cultural differences	Unit 4 Unit 5
7 COURSES	uncountable nouns ending in *s* relative clauses adjective + infinitive modals of obligation *ask/tell* + object + infinitive	education: subjects, courses, exams household activities	turning points in your education training to be a butler what do people do at acting school?	Unit 5 Unit 6
8 ALL IN A DAY'S WORK	link words: concession and addition making and refusing requests asking for / refusing permission	work verb + noun collocations fixed phrases	role playing work situations pros and cons of being self-employed different managerial styles	Unit 6 Unit 7
9 FROM THE CRADLE TO THE GRAVE	obligation, prohibition and permission present simple passive	ages and stages in life birth, marriage and death	what people think about at different stages laws and customs weddings in different cultures	Unit 7 Unit 8
10 PHONAHOLICS	*used to* + infinitive and *would* + infinitive for past habits what to say on the phone	telephoning phrasal verbs hobbies synonyms	personal telephone questionnaire predicting phone conversations being a phone addict	Unit 8 Unit 9
11 GOODS AND SERVICES	*if* sentences with *will* and *might* *to have something done*	shopping electrical appliances and consumer goods suffixes	are you a good salesperson? services in different countries products and their benefits	Unit 9 Unit 10

Unit	Language focus	Vocabulary	Topics	Review
12 BARE NECESSITIES	frequency and degree adverbs describing need qualifying adjectives	climate and geography personal belongings numbers and measurements	what do you keep under the bed? unusual hotels air travel	Unit 10 Unit 11
13 WHO IS REALLY ON TRIAL?	*if* sentences with *would* and *might* relative clauses link words: similarities and differences	crime law the legal system	crime prevention advice from an ex-criminal for and against juries	Unit 11 Unit 12
14 TALL STORIES, SHORT STORIES	past perfect simple apologising making excuses and reassuring purpose, reason, result	the countryside action verbs transport	telling stories making up good excuses	Unit 12 Unit 13
15 LOVE THY NEIGHBOUR	verb patterns present perfect simple and continuous	guessing words in context reporting verbs	being kind for no reason what makes a good group noisy neighbours	Unit 13 Unit 14
16 YES AND NO	saying *no* politely forming negatives *wish* + past simple *if* sentences with *would* and *might* *something, anything, nothing*	negative prefixes negative adverbs	saying *no* in different cultures a 'negatives' quiz positive thinking	Unit 14 Unit 15
17 PACKAGING	partitives numbers and quantities making associations, e.g. *makes me think of ...*	containers food money abstract nouns holidays	arranging holidays advertising	Unit 15 Unit 16
18 HONESTLY SPEAKING	reported speech reported questions reporting verbs	reporting verbs politics and economics triumphs and disasters	Dorothy Parker short story how honest are you? is there too much bad news in the news?	Unit 16 Unit 17
19 PLAIN ENGLISH	formal and informal English *should, ought to* and *had better* verb + *-ing* form preposition + *-ing* form adjective + infinitive	bureaucracy symptoms of fear adjectives	writing simple English how to write a good CV public speaking	Unit 17 Unit 18
20 ART AND SOCIETY	passives modal passives revision of link words articles	art everyday objects	art and design story of a court artist history of money	Unit 18 Unit 19
21 DARE YOURSELF TO SUCCEED	*should have* + past participle past conditional	work outdoor activities verb/adjective + prepositions	applying for jobs 'white' lies executive training courses talking about past success and failure	Unit 19 Unit 20
22 FORCES OF NATURE	*used to* + infinitive vs. *be used to* + *-ing* form *if* and *unless*	health and natural remedies abstract nouns word building	living through an earthquake homeopathic medicine *feng shui*	Unit 20 Unit 21

LOOKING BACK AND LOOKING FORWARD

Language focus:	Vocabulary:
past simple revision	memories and recollections
will for prediction	adjectives describing emotions
different uses of the present continuous	learning and revision

I CAN VAGUELY REMEMBER ...   past simple revision; adjectives of emotion

1 Which of these firsts can you remember? Have there been other important firsts in your life? Tell a partner, using the language in the box to help you.

I can't remember .... at all.
I can vaguely remember ....
I can remember .... quite well.
I can remember .... very clearly.

- your first English lesson
- your first attempts at driving
- your first pay cheque
- your first room or flat
- the first time you used English outside class
- the first time you met your boss
- the first time you went on holiday without your parents
- your first day at primary school
- your first kiss
- the first record, cassette or CD you bought
- the first time you realised that adults weren't always right

Other important firsts: ....
....
....

2 Check that you understand and can pronounce the words in the box. Use a dictionary or ask a partner or your teacher.

> excited   nervous   scared stiff   relaxed   worried   surprised
> disappointed   upset   great   awful   embarrassed   confident
> delighted   shocked

Work in small groups. Choose some of the *firsts* from Exercise 1, and say how you felt, and why.

Example: *I can remember my first English lesson very clearly. I felt a bit nervous because I didn't know any of the other learners, but by the end of the lesson I started to feel more relaxed. It was quite fun, in fact.*

3 〇〇 〇〇 The double 〇〇 here and in other parts of the book means that there are two recordings of the listening: an easier one, and a more difficult one. Decide which one to listen to, or listen to both.

Listen to the speakers on the recording talking about their memories. Which of the topics in Exercise 1 are they talking about, and what happened? Make notes.

4 Compare your notes with your partner. How do you think the speakers felt? Use adjectives from Exercise 2.

HOW TIMES HAVE CHANGED   *will* for prediction; past simple

1 Answer these questions in groups.

- What year was it 20 years ago?
- What important events can you remember around that time:
  a. in your country?
  b. in the rest of the world?
  c. in your family?
- In general, was it a good time or a bad time?

2 Underline any new words or phrases in this list. Check the meaning in a dictionary, or ask your partner.

Twenty years ago …
- people worked longer hours than they do today.
- most people didn't go abroad for their holidays.
- people wrote most things by hand.
- most people looked after their elderly relatives.
- people didn't have central heating or air conditioning in their homes.
- there wasn't any terrorism.
- people smoked a lot more.
- people only ate fruit and vegetables in season.
- there were more communist countries.
- people listened to music on records and cassettes.
- people committed fewer serious crimes.
- everyone was healthier than they are today.
- people had more false teeth.
- most people didn't learn English at school.
- drivers could always find a parking space.
- people didn't use computers.

3 Look at the list again. Which sentences are mostly true and which are mostly false about life 20 years ago? Discuss in small groups.

4 What about the things in the list 20 years from now? Work in small groups and say what you believe will happen in the future using these structures:

will + verb   *won't (= will not)* + verb   *(I don't think) … will* + verb

Examples: *I think people will work fewer hours than now.*
I don't think people will listen to records or cassettes: they'll listen to compact discs.
Most people won't write things by hand at all: they'll use computers.

5 Read the two texts. Notice the time expressions in **bold**.

In the past, you could find a parking space easily in town. But people often parked where they wanted, so there were a lot of traffic jams. **Nowadays**, it is very hard to park in town; there are too many cars on the road and not enough car parks or parking meters. **In the future**, people will have to use public transport much more. They won't be able to drive into the centre of many towns.

In the past, people wrote many things by hand, but they also used typewriters a lot for more formal documents. **Nowadays**, children learn to use computers from an early age, and few people use typewriters. With credit cards, we don't even write as many cheques by hand. **In the future**, people will probably depend on technology more and more, and some people won't need to write anything by hand.

Underline the verbs in the two texts. Which tenses are used here:

1. after *in the past*?   2. after *nowadays*?   3. after *in the future*?

Work with a partner. Choose one of the topics from the list in Exercise 2, and write a paragraph similar to the ones above. When you have finished, show your paragraph to others, or put it on the wall for other people to read.

1 Read the dialogues below. Which dialogue goes with each of these pictures?

1. A: Hi! I haven't seen you for ages! How are things?
   B: Fine. How about you?
   A: Not bad. I finally decided to leave the post office. Ten years behind a counter is enough for anyone. I'm working at the hospital in the casualty department at the moment, but I'm looking for another job.

   B: ....

   A: ....

a

2. A: Hello?
   B: Hi, Carly. It's Arthur.
   A: Hi. How are you?
   B: Fine. Look, Carly, I haven't got long because I'm working at the hospital right now, and my boss hates me using the phone. But can we meet after work?
   A: All right. I'll meet you in the usual place then.

   B: ....

   A: ....

b

3. A: So, David, can you repair the roof for us, then?
   B: Oh, yes – I'd like the work.
   A: How about next Monday?
   B: Sorry, I can't: I'm working at the hospital all week. And I can't change that obviously because we fixed it up months ago ...

   A: ....

   B: ....

c

2 Work with your partner. Continue the dialogues with two more lines. Then read one of your dialogues to another pair.

3 The present continuous (***I'm working** at the hospital*) is used in all three dialogues, but the meaning is different. Which example describes:

1. something happening at the exact moment of speaking?
2. a future arrangement?★
3. something temporary which is not necessarily happening at the moment of speaking?

★ something that has been agreed or organised for the future

Compare your answers with a partner.

4 Write sentences in the table, using the present continuous with different meanings. Here are some topics you could write about:

family   leisure   holidays
work/study   accommodation   finance
health and fitness   transport   possessions

1. *happening at this exact moment*
   a. *My wife is studying in the class next door.*
   b. ....
   c. ....

2. *arrangements made about the future*
   a. *I'm having dinner with my sister next week.*
   b. ....
   c. ....

3. *something temporary, not necessarily happening at the moment of speaking*
   a. *I'm trying to find a new job.*
   b. ....
   c. ....

Work with a partner. Read out your sentences in a different order. Your partner should say which use you intend for each one.

Example: YOU: *I'm wearing my father's watch.*
             YOUR PARTNER: *Happening at this exact moment?*
             YOU: *That's right.*

5 Work with a partner and look at the pairs of sentences. In each pair, is one sentence correct or are they both correct?

1. a. Could you come back later? I'm working.
   b. Could you come back later? I work.

2. a. They build a new library next to our college.
   b. They are building a new library next to our college.

3. a. She's leaving at midnight tonight.
   b. She's going to leave at midnight tonight.

4. a. I think it's raining tomorrow.
   b. I think it will rain tomorrow.

5. a. I can't see you tonight because I'm having dinner with some clients.
   b. I can't see you tonight because I'll have dinner with some clients.

REVIEW AND DEVELOPMENT
vocabulary: learning methods; revision

1 Read this short text. Do you disagree with any of it? If so, tell the class.

> If you just see a word once, or you learn a bit of grammar once, there is a good chance that you will soon forget it. That is not because you are a bad learner. It is a simple fact of learning that if you recall words, phrases and structures from your memory and use them, it gets easier the next time you need this language. In other words, you need to come back to things you have learnt once and revise them. Often this can be done very quickly, but 'little and often' is a useful expression when it comes to learning.

2 Here are some different things learners do. Find a word or phrase with the same meaning as *revise* in each one.

Well, I tend to have another look at my notes or the book on the way to my English class.

I go back and look at the book or my notes every night before I go to bed.

I try to review everything we learn, but I find it boring and I give up easily.

I go over the lessons in my book at the end of every unit.

I occasionally look through my notes again but I find it discouraging. It just shows me how much I've forgotten.

Tick any sentences above which are true for you, or write your own. Compare your answers in small groups.

3 Write a list of ways you can revise, using the pictures and your own ideas.

Example: *You can copy words from the coursebook into a vocabulary notebook, and then try to memorise them.*

Tell the class all the other ideas you had for revising.

4 🔲 Listen to the speakers on the recording. Do they include any of the things in your list? Make a note of any other ideas they give.

Now work in groups. Tell others which you think are the best ideas. Do you think the same strategies work for everybody, or is revising a very personal matter?

5 Now look again at the first three parts of this unit. Which revision ideas would be suitable for any of the material? Compare your answers with a partner.

PERSONAL STUDY WORKBOOK

In your Personal Study Workbook, you will find more exercises to help you with your learning. For Unit 1, these include:

- vocabulary activities on synonyms and topic groups
- a writing exercise using different tenses
- pronunciation work on word stress
- reading and listening passages about memories and events in history
- your first speaking partners activity
- a page on street vocabulary in your visual dictionary

HOW DOES THAT SOUND?

Language focus:	Vocabulary:
comparative structures	ways of talking
countable and uncountable nouns	adjectives
pronunciation	class words, e.g. *furniture, toys*

HOW DO YOU SOUND IN ENGLISH?

1 Read the definitions in the box, then answer the questions below in groups.

Sounds are	vowels. Example: /iː/, /ɪ/
	diphthongs: two vowel sounds together. Example: /eɪ/
	consonants. Example: /k/, /ʃ/
A *syllable* is	part of a word that contains a vowel sound. Example: *dog* has one syllable, *return* has two syllables, *computer* has three syllables.
Stress is	the emphasis you put on a syllable, so that it sounds a bit louder.
	Example: in the word *decide* 'cide' is louder.
Rhythm is	the regular repetition of stressed syllables. Example: *He offered to buy me a cup of coffee.*
Intonation is	the rise and fall in the level of your voice when you are speaking.
	Example: *Would you like some cake? Thank you.*

1. What is very different about English pronunciation from that of your own language?
2. What do you find most difficult about English pronunciation?
3. Do you have any special ways of improving your pronunciation? Tell the class any special ways you use.

/aː/   /uː/   /iː/

---

2 ⬚⬚ ⬚⬚ Clare Fletcher is a teacher and pronunciation expert. Listen to the recording and make notes on the advice she gives for improving your pronunciation out of class.

Which is the most useful advice for you? Discuss in groups.

3 Clare suggests that you can improve your pronunciation most quickly by working on stress. Dictionaries show you where the stress falls, but they do it in different ways.

NOUN, PERSONAL PRONOUN
pro·nounce /prəˈnaʊns/ *v* **1** [T] to make the sound of (a letter, a word, etc.): *In the word "knew", the "k" is not pronounced.* | *How do you pronounce your name?* **2** [T+obj+adj/n] to declare, esp. officially or after consideration: *The doctor pronounced the man dead.* | Th...

pronounce /prəˈnaʊns/, pronounces, pronouncing, pronounced. 1 To pronounce a v·o,or v·o·o word or sound means to say it in a particular way, usually in the accepted way for a particular language. *We can never be certain in English how an...*

You can also mark it with boxes above the word, like this: pronou̇nce

Learners often have difficulty with word stress on the items in the boxes below. Work with a partner and mark the stress, as in the examples.

Jobs	*Countries*	*Concrete nouns*	*Abstract nouns*	*Adjectives*
policeman	Italy	vegetable	development	necessary
engineer	Japan	calculator	industry	interesting
professor	Egypt	magazine	advantages	reliable
secretary	Brazil	certificate	career	Arabic
photographer	Iran	machine	democracy	comfortable

Practise saying the words correctly with your partner.

4 Complete any five of these sentences using words from Exercise 3.

I wouldn't like to be .a policeman............................... .

I've never been to .... but I'd like to.

I've got to go and buy ....

I don't know very much about ....

My car is ....

I'm a bit worried about ....

Do you know anyone who is .... ?

5 Practise saying your sentences naturally, then tell them to a partner. See if your partner can repeat them back to you without reading them.

1 📼 Listen to the recording. What are the people doing? Use the words in the box.

scream	mumble
whisper	shout
yell	whistle
cry	cheer

Example: *1. Someone is shouting.*

2 Complete these sentences in a suitable way and then compare in small groups.

People sometimes scream when ....

They usually cry if ....

They sometimes shout if ....

They usually whisper when ....

They might yell if ....

They usually cheer when ....

They often whistle when ....

Some people mumble if ....

Now tell a partner about yourself using the words, like this:

Example: *The last time I screamed was when I saw someone run in front of a car in the road. I thought it was going to hit him, but it didn't.*
I never whistle; I can't.

3 When we are comparing things, we often use comparative adjectives (adjective + *-er*, or *more* + adjective).

Are these sentences correct? If not, change them. You can check with the Grammar Reference on page 159 if you aren't sure of the rules.

1. His voice is more loud than mine.
2. This lecture was more interesting than last week's.
3. She has a terrible cough. It's more bad than mine.
4. We were calmer after seeing the doctor.
5. She's better that the other assistant.
6. She's got a softer voice than the others.
7. The children are more happy now.
8. He was more anxious than I had expected.

You can also modify a comparative, like this:

The first voice is	a bit much far a great deal	more interesting softer nicer calmer more attractive	than the second.

4 🎧 Listen to the pairs of sentences. After each one, compare the two sentences with a partner, using the structures in Exercise 3.

Example: *1. The speaker in the second sentence is* **much louder than** *the speaker in the first.*

5 Write down three sentences or questions as in the recording. Then work in small groups. Say each sentence in two different ways. See if your group can identify how you said them.

Example: *In the first sentence your voice was much calmer.*

DOES IT MAKE A NOISE?
uncountable nouns; class words

1 Work with a partner and use a dictionary to check the meaning and word stress of any new words in the box.

> toy   furniture   bomb   room   experience   lorry   weather
> luggage   electric drill   time   research   training   hair   scenery
> accommodation   machinery   toast   hammer   equipment   traffic
> advice   paper   air conditioning   work

2 🎧 Work with your partner. Listen to the quiz on the recording. Write your answers and then compare with another pair.

3 A good dictionary will tell you if words are countable, uncountable, or both. Look at these examples from different dictionaries.

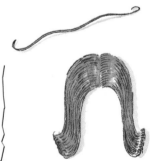

it nails.
hair /heə/, **hairs**. 1 A **hair** is one of the long, fine, N COUNT thread-like things that grows in large numbers on ᵗ strand the top part of your head and on other parts of your body. Hair also grows on the bodies of some other animals. EG ...*black hairs on the back of his hands...* *Its underside is naked except for a few sparse hairs.*
▸ Your **hair** is the large number of hairs that grow in ▸ N UNCOUNT a mass on your head. EG ...*a young woman with long* ᵗ strands *blonde hair... I washed my hands and combed my hair. ...hair lotion.*

tall of HAIR
hair /£heər, $her/ *n* the mass of thin threadlike structures on the head of a person, or any of these structures that grow out of the skin of a person or animal ● *He's got short dark hair.* [U] ● *I'm going to have my hair cut.* [U] ● *He watched as she brushed her long red hair.* [U] ● *He had lost his hair by the time he was twenty-five.* [U] ● *My husband is like a monkey – he's even got hair on his back!* [U] ● *He's starting to get a few grey hairs now.* [C] ● *I found a hair in my soup.* [C] ● *My grandmother has long dark hairs growing out of her nose.* [C] ● *The antelope had a tuft of hair on its*

4 Organise the words from Exercise 1 into these categories. Work with a partner and use dictionaries to help you.

1. *Nouns which are always countable*
   Example: *a toy / toys*   *We'll give her a toy / some toys for her birthday.*
2. *Nouns which are always uncountable*
   Example: *furniture*   *They've got some new furniture and it's horrible.*
        (Notice the verb is singular, and furniture doesn't take an *s*.)
3. *Nouns which can be countable or uncountable*
   Example: *hair*   *She's got beautiful hair.* (uncountable)
              There's a hair in my soup. (countable)

5 Make these sentences plural where possible.

          They were   some hammers
Example: ~~He was~~ buying ~~a hammer~~ and some sports equipment.

1. The weather's very bad at the moment.
2. I put my luggage next to the escalator.
3. His advice was very helpful.
4. Is your toast burnt?
5. The lorry was destroyed by the bomb.
6. There isn't enough room for the machinery.
7. Has she had any training for this work?
8. His research involved special equipment.

6 Work in groups of four. One pair in each group should complete table 1 while the other pair completes table 2. Use words from the lesson or any others.

1.	*Countable noun*	*Uncountable noun*
something that makes no noise at all	....	....
something that makes a slight noise if you drop it	....	....
something that makes a noise you don't like	....	....

2.	*Countable noun*	*Uncountable noun*
a sound which reminds you of a season	....	....
something that makes a noise in the street	....	....
something that makes a quiet continuous noise	....	....

Show the other pair your answers. Do they think your words are appropriate and correct?

PERSONAL STUDY WORKBOOK

In your Personal Study Workbook, you will find more exercises to help you with your learning. For Unit 2, these include:

- exercises on uncountable nouns and comparative and superlative structures
- listening to public announcements in different places
- pronunciation work on weak forms
- writing a story from sounds
- another page of your visual dictionary to complete – groups of objects

---

REVIEW OF UNIT 1

1 Bingo! | irregular past tenses |

A Complete the table, putting the past form of any 15 of the verbs from the list in the spaces.

brought		

become	bite	bleed	~~bring~~	burn
catch	choose	cost	dream	fall
feel	fly	grow	hear	hide	hurt
keep	lend	let	mean	ride
shake	sing	smell	spend	stand
steal	throw	wear	win	

B ☐☐ Listen to the recording. When you hear one of your verbs in a sentence, cross it out in your table. When you have completed one column of five verbs, shout 'Bingo!'. You are the winner.

2 What's the missing preposition? | vocabulary |

Prepositions form an important part of many verbs and phrases. Complete these sentences with the correct preposition to form a phrase or verb.

1. We only eat vegetables .... season.
2. I didn't like the film .... all.
3. I'm not looking forward .... Monday morning.
4. Could you look .... the children while I go shopping?
5. .... general people don't write many things .... hand.
6. The couple get married .... the end of the book.
7. I'm afraid the manager is away .... holiday right now.
8. .... the past many homes didn't have central heating. .... fact, they didn't have much heating .... all.

The verbs and phrases are in Unit 1, so look through the unit and find them to check your answers. Work with a partner.

3 How to say -ed endings | pronunciation |

☐☐ How do you pronounce the final -ed in these words? Is it /t/ or /d/, or /ɪd/? Put the words into the correct columns below and then listen to check your answers.

embarrassed	excited	scared	surprised	delighted	relaxed
interested	shocked	frightened	disappointed	confused	astonished

	/t/ or /d/	/ɪd/
Examples:	*worked*	*started*
	lived	....
	....	....
	....	....
	....	....

Test each other on your pronunciation of the words.
Can you see any rule or pattern for these -ed endings? Discuss in small groups.

GAMES PEOPLE PLAY

Language focus:
expressing likes and dislikes,
preferences and opinions
verb + *-ing* form or infinitive
preposition + *-ing*
defining and paraphrasing

Vocabulary:
sport and leisure activities
verbs and adjectives + prepositions
character

I'M NOT VERY KEEN ON IT
sports vocabulary; giving opinions

1 Work with a partner. Write down answers to these questions, and try not to repeat the same sport twice.

Can you name …
- five sports that don't use a ball?
- four sports ending in *-ball*?
- three sports played on a court?
- two sports that use a track?
- two sports that use a table?
- one sport that uses a ring?
- one sport where you use a set of clubs?

2 Do you think these sentences about sports express positive opinions, negative opinions or are they neutral? Write *P*, *N* or *Neut.*

1. Personally I think it's barbaric.
2. You have to be incredibly fit if you want to be good at it.
3. I think it's terrific.
4. I can't see the point of it at all.
5. It requires a lot of skill.
6. I can't stand it.
7. It's my favourite sport.
8. The rules are far too complicated.
9. It's quite hard but very stimulating.
10. I've never tried it.
11. I find it far too competitive.
12. I'm not very keen on it.

3 Do any of the sentences express *your* opinion about particular sports? Write the sport next to each sentence, and then discuss your opinions in groups.

4 Match the leisure activities in the photographs with the words in the box.

> playing cards   crossword puzzles
> dominoes   backgammon   pinball
> Monopoly   chess   majong

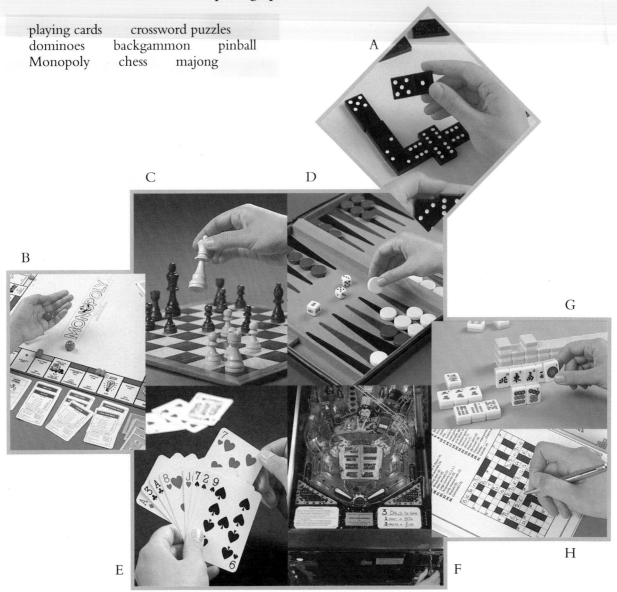

Are they usually done/played by men, women or both? Discuss with a partner.
Did you find any interesting answers? How do you explain them?

5 Work in groups. Give your opinions about the leisure activities in the pictures, if possible using some of the expressions from Exercise 2.

6 Tell your group about any other sports or activities you do yourself.

I NEVER LIKED GAMES AT SCHOOL   verb + *-ing* form or infinitive; preposition + *-ing*

1 People sometimes change their minds. Can you think of games or sports that you like now but didn't like when you were younger, or vice versa? Why have you changed your mind? Discuss in small groups.

2 🎧 Listen to these people talking about different activities and complete each text.

Max
I tried to avoid .... when I was at school, and I
absolutely refused .... such as
rugby or football. I could never understand why other boys wanted
.... on a cold, wet, windy afternoon in the
middle of winter. But my two sons adore football, and I quite enjoy
.... for their school teams.

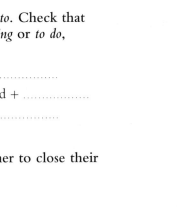

Jean
I decided .... because friends of mine
played. At first it was just for fun and I wasn't interested in
.... Gradually though, as I improved, I became
more and more competitive. Now I can't stand ....

Patrick
I used to be afraid of ...., then I met a
couple of people who spent every weekend ....
.................:...... and they persuaded me .... At
first I was terrified but gradually I overcame my fear, and now I
can't imagine ....

Sally
Not long ago I decided it was time I learnt ....
I've always felt embarrassed that I couldn't, and I was worried about
.... I did quite well,
and after a few lessons, I managed .... It
made me feel really great!

Compare your answers with a partner.

3 Some verbs are followed by an *-ing* form, others by an infinitive with *to*. Check that
you understand the verbs below, then try to complete the list with *doing* or *to do*,
without looking back at Exercise 2.

decide + *to do* ....   spend (time) + ...   want + ...
avoid + ...   refuse + ...   can't stand + ...
enjoy + ...   persuade somebody + ...   learn + ...
manage + ...   imagine + ...

Look back at Exercise 2 and check your answers. Then tell your partner to close their
book and test them.

4 There are three other *-ing* forms in Exercise 2. Find them and discuss with a partner
why the *-ing* form is used.

5 Write a short paragraph about yourself, similar to the ones in Exercise 2. Include at least three of the *-ing* form or infinitive constructions. Then work in small groups. Listen to each person read out their paragraph, and ask them more questions about what they said.

1 Look at the titles and photos of TV game shows. Can you guess what the game is in each case? Do you have similar games on TV in your country? Compare your answers in groups.

Mastermind

The Price is Right

Family Fortunes

A Question of Sport

2 What sort of people do well on TV game shows, in your opinion? With a partner, make a list of possible characteristics.

Example: *people who are confident*

Compare your answers with the information in the text below.

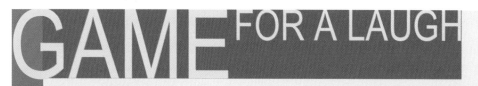

GAME FOR A LAUGH

HAVE YOU EVER THOUGHT of going on a TV quiz show? The games are played for a laugh, but the prizes can be really fabulous: cars, stereos, TVs, videos and exotic holidays.

Of course, being a game show contestant is not for everyone. Fear of the camera is a common worry, and general shyness is another. But for those who *are* keen, Christine Patterson from a leading independent TV production company has some advice.

'Contestants need to be quick-witted, fast on the buzzer and not shy about appearing on TV. They can be aged from 18 to 80 to compete.' She also believes that 'you need to have a reasonable amount of general knowledge, but an important factor is how your personality shows itself on TV.'

Do you have to be confident?

'If you can talk freely and are confident,' says Christine, 'it's an advantage.'

Most contestants agree that being on quiz shows is addictive. It's frightening and nerve-racking. But once you've done it, you just want to go back and do it again and again.

If you have read this far and still think you would like to be a contestant, you have made a very revealing statement about yourself. You are bright, bored, not afraid to look silly in front of others, and almost certainly an eternal optimist. Pessimists, who may have all the other qualities, rarely enter game shows, saying 'What's the point? I wouldn't win anything.'

Which are you?

In your class, who do you think would make good game show contestants?

3 You are going to take part in a game show. But first, match the definitions with the words in the box.

It means the same as *very frightened*.
It's the opposite of *awful*.
It's a kind/type of board game.
It's (the place) where you borrow books.
It's someone who designs buildings.
It's the thing you use for locking a door.
It's the stuff you use to protect your skin in the summer.

fantastic   key   library   chess   suntan lotion   architect   scared stiff

4 ☐☐ Listen to two people playing a word game. One person has a list of words, which he has to explain or define to the other person, who must then guess the word. Tick any sentence beginnings you hear from Exercise 3. Then compare with a partner.

5 ☐☐ Now listen to the second recording. Try to guess the words being defined, and shout out your answers.

6 Organise yourselves into teams. Your teacher will give one of you some words to define. The winning team is the one which guesses the highest number of words in the quickest time.

PERSONAL STUDY WORKBOOK

In your Personal Study Workbook, you will find more exercises to help you with your learning. For Unit 3, these include:

• an exercise to test yourself on *-ing* forms and infinitives
• a word building exercise
• a pronunciation exercise on connected speech
• a text about women in sport
• another page of your visual dictionary to complete – games and sports

REVIEW OF UNIT 1

1 Correct my mistakes | verb forms |

A ▭ Each sentence on the recording contains a mistake. First, write down the sentences you hear, including the mistakes.

B Now correct the sentences and read them to a partner.

2 Choose the right emotion | adjectives |

Choose a suitable adjective from the box to complete each of the sentences below. More than one answer may be possible.

> nervous   worried   pleased   scared stiff   little   upset   shocked
> delighted   embarrassed   vague   afraid   great

1. I was very .... when she said she didn't want to come to my party.
2. When my husband didn't come home from work yesterday, I was very ....
3. We had a lovely time in Kenya and it was .... to go back and see old friends.
4. I was alone in the house, so when I heard a noise coming from upstairs I was absolutely ....
5. I have a .... memory of going to Australia, but I was only seven at the time.
6. He hates exams and he always gets very .... before an important one.
7. I gave her a lovely bouquet of flowers for her birthday, and then she told me that her birthday was the 16th of April and not the 16th of March. I felt very ....
8. I was .... when she told me she'd got the job because I knew it was very important to her.

REVIEW OF UNIT 2

1 On the piste | countable and uncountable nouns |

Read part of a letter and then do the exercise on the next page.

> *Getting around the city was easy because there were plenty of buses and trams, and they nearly always ran on time. But when we went up to the skiing resort, it took us ages to get there because the roads were quite narrow and there were some awful jams. But it was worth it. The place was just fabulous; there were snow-covered peaks all around us, and the views were spectacular.*
>
> *Our chalet was also quite spacious, and it had an excellent fitted kitchen and modern bathroom. However, the bed wasn't the most comfortable in the world, and we both felt that the sofa and armchairs did not encourage relaxation at the end of a day's skiing.*
>
> *And for beginners, we did quite well. Not as well as some of the children, of course. They picked it up so easily, and by the end of the holiday were incredibly good. Anyway, we hired the skis and all the other stuff – it cost a fortune as you predicted – and had some lessons from a very nice instructor. He was very patient with everyone and we were astonished at the way some people blamed him every time they fell over. It was stupid of them and quite unnecessary.*
>
> *We were on the slopes all day and very lucky that it was cold and sunny most of the time – ideal for skiing. The travel agency had suggested going this time of year, and in our case they were absolutely right.*

Complete the sentences with the writer's thoughts and opinions. (Try not to use the words in the letter.)

Example: *accommodation*
He thought the accommodation was good.

1. He thought the public transport ....
2. He thought the furniture ....
3. The weather ....
4. He thought the scenery ....
5. The children ....
6. He thought the traffic ....
7. The equipment they hired ....
8. He felt that some of the people in the skiing class ....
9. He thought the advice given to them at the travel agency ....

2 Picture box | comparatives and superlatives |

Work in small groups. Take turns to make statements about the things in the pictures, using these structures and any adjectives you like:

	a bit		
X is	much	(bigger)	than Y.
	far	(more expensive)	
	a great deal		

| Z is | the (silliest) | thing in the pictures. |
| | the (most unusual) | |

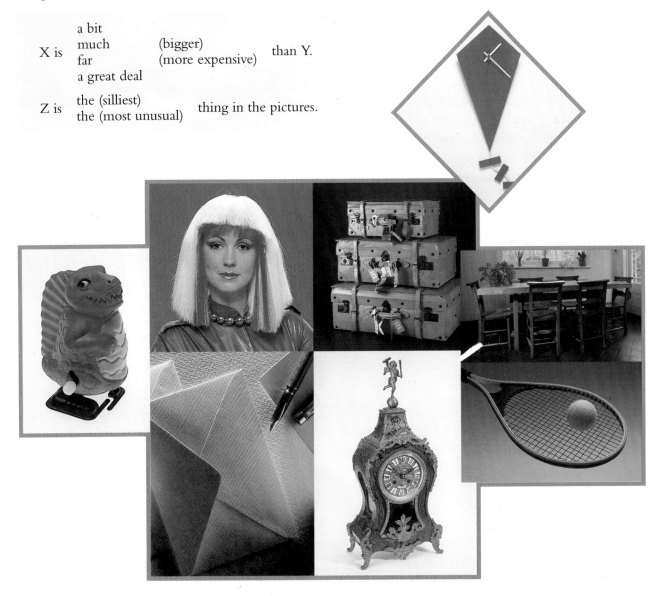

If you disagree with someone's statement, say why. Continue until you have mentioned all the things.

4

NEWSPAPERS AND MAGAZINES

Language focus:	Vocabulary:
past simple and present perfect	newspapers
for, since and *yet*	social issues
verb + preposition	adjectives describing people

1 Work with a partner. Use a dictionary to check the underlined words below, then decide if the sentences are true or false. If false, correct them.

1. Journalists, reporters and editors are all members of the Press.
2. An editor usually writes articles for newspapers.
3. Most journalists are always looking for a scoop.
4. The circulation of a newspaper means the number of copies it sells.
5. British tabloid newspapers have long articles and few photographs.
6. A caption is a kind of article.

With your partner, choose two of the words below and write sentences (true or false) about them, as in the exercise above.

    a headline   a scandal   a broadsheet   a column

Show your sentences to another pair. Do they think they are true or false?

2 Look at the contents page of the newspaper in the red box, then discuss these questions in small groups.

1. Do newspapers in your country include all these sections?
2. Do newspapers in your country include other sections? If so, what?
3. Look at the number of pages for each section in the newspaper below. Is it the same or different in newspapers in your country?
4. Are there any other sections you would like to see in a daily paper?

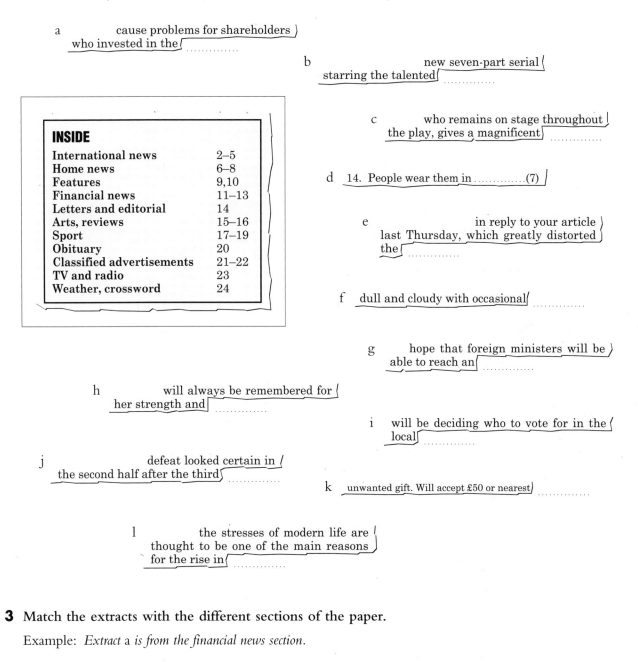

a   cause problems for shareholders who invested in the ....

b   new seven-part serial starring the talented ....

INSIDE

International news	2–5
Home news	6–8
Features	9,10
Financial news	11–13
Letters and editorial	14
Arts, reviews	15–16
Sport	17–19
Obituary	20
Classified advertisements	21–22
TV and radio	23
Weather, crossword	24

c   who remains on stage throughout the play, gives a magnificent ....

d   14. People wear them in ....(7)

e   in reply to your article last Thursday, which greatly distorted the ....

f   dull and cloudy with occasional ....

g   hope that foreign ministers will be able to reach an ....

h   will always be remembered for her strength and ....

i   will be deciding who to vote for in the local ....

j   defeat looked certain in the second half after the third ....

k   unwanted gift. Will accept £50 or nearest ....

l   the stresses of modern life are thought to be one of the main reasons for the rise in ....

3 Match the extracts with the different sections of the paper.

Example: *Extract a is from the financial news section.*

4 Work with a partner. Complete the extracts with a word from the box.

goal   divorce   bed   showers   agreement   courage   election
company   actress   facts   performance   offer

5 Choose one of the extracts and write the next sentence. Show it to a partner. Can they identify the extract?

1 What's your favourite magazine, and why? Discuss with a partner.

2 Find out more about people's attitudes to magazines. Complete this survey and then discuss your answers in groups.

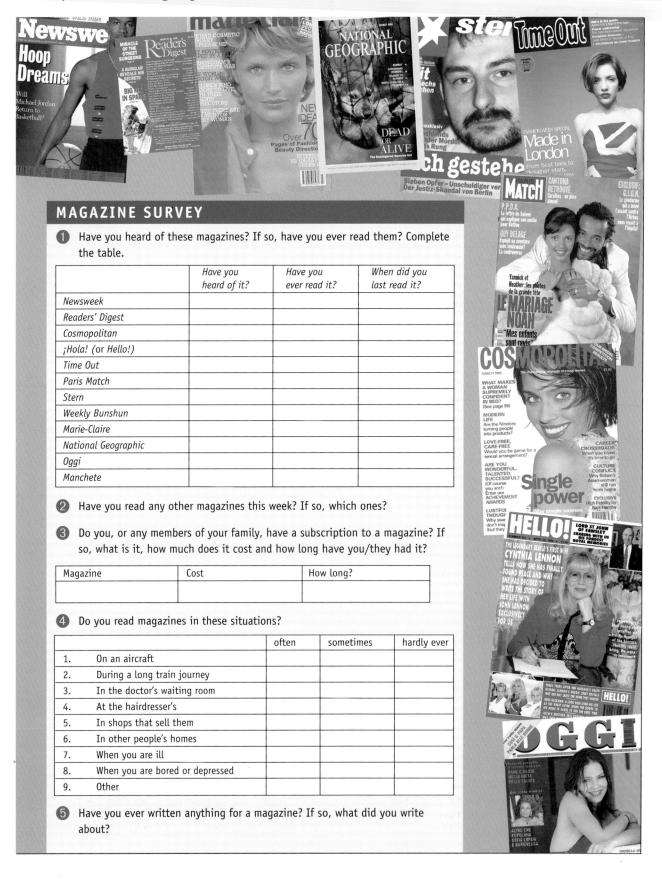

MAGAZINE SURVEY

❶ Have you heard of these magazines? If so, have you ever read them? Complete the table.

	Have you heard of it?	Have you ever read it?	When did you last read it?
Newsweek			
Readers' Digest			
Cosmopolitan			
¡Hola! (or Hello!)			
Time Out			
Paris Match			
Stern			
Weekly Bunshun			
Marie-Claire			
National Geographic			
Oggi			
Manchete			

❷ Have you read any other magazines this week? If so, which ones?

❸ Do you, or any members of your family, have a subscription to a magazine? If so, what is it, how much does it cost and how long have you/they had it?

Magazine	Cost	How long?

❹ Do you read magazines in these situations?

		often	sometimes	hardly ever
1.	On an aircraft			
2.	During a long train journey			
3.	In the doctor's waiting room			
4.	At the hairdresser's			
5.	In shops that sell them			
6.	In other people's homes			
7.	When you are ill			
8.	When you are bored or depressed			
9.	Other			

❺ Have you ever written anything for a magazine? If so, what did you write about?

3 Look back through the survey and underline all the examples of the past simple and the present perfect simple.

Examples: *When <u>did you read</u> it?* (past simple)   *<u>Have you heard</u> of it?* (present perfect)

Read these descriptions of different uses of the present perfect, then write down an example for each one from the survey.

1. To ask or talk about something in the past without saying when it happened.
2. To ask or talk about an action or situation in a period of time that hasn't finished.
3. To ask or talk about an action or situation which began in the past and continues up to the present.

4 Now look at the examples of the past simple in the speech bubbles. Can you explain why it is used in each one, and how it is different in meaning from the examples of the present perfect?

I bought two magazines yesterday but I haven't read them.

1

I've read hundreds of books in my first language, but last week I read a whole book in English.

2

3

I've kept these magazines for about ten years. Before that I always threw them away.

5 Put the verb in brackets into the correct form. Then compare with a partner.

1 My brother (work) on several different magazines. He (start) with a magazine for motorcycling enthusiasts, and then he (move) to a car magazine where he (write) a weekly article about car security. He (enjoy) it but (leave) five years ago to work on a new men's magazine. He (be) there ever since, and last year he (become) Deputy Editor.

2 A: You (write) your article yet?
B: Yes I (finish) it a couple of days ago.
A: The editor (see) it?
B: No, not yet. But I'm seeing him tomorrow.

3 A: What does he do?
B: He owns The Daily Record, so he's a powerful man.
A: Really? How long he (have) that?
B: I think it (be) in the family for over fifty years.
A: As long as that?
B: Yes, his grandfather (buy) it in the 1940s.

6 Complete these sentences about yourself in a logical way, using the past simple or present perfect simple.

1. .... yesterday.
2. .... since 1990.
3. .... all my life.
4. .... three weeks ago.
5. .... last week.
6. .... for the last ten years.
7. .... in 1993.
8. .... yet.
9. .... since I was a child.
10. .... when I was a child.

Compare your sentences in small groups.

1 How much do you know about the Spanish magazine *¡Hola!* and *Hello!* (the British version)? Tell a partner.

2 ⬚⬚ ⬚⬚ Listen to the recording and complete these sentences about the two magazines.

1. *¡Hola!* started in ....
2. Since 1984, Eduardo Sánchez Junco ....
3. It sells .... copies a week and makes an annual profit of
   ....
4. Famous people are happy to be interviewed by *¡Hola!* because ....
   ....
5. The British version, *Hello!*, started in ....
6. It began to make a profit by ....
7. Since then ....
8. *Hello!* only gets .... of its revenue from advertising.

Compare your answers with a partner.

3 Look at the readership profiles for the two magazines below. Think about the readership of *¡Hola!/Hello!* and write a similar profile.

Mainly For Men
A magazine aimed primarily at professional men in their twenties and early thirties. The magazine believes most of their readers are interested in fashion, but also want in-depth articles and interviews. In other words, serious but not too intellectual. The editor would also like to attract more female readers, but without losing their male readers.

Hers
A magazine mostly for women in the 25–45 age range. Very few men buy the magazine, but quite a lot read it. The magazine is primarily aimed at women who work, but it seems to attract women from a wide range of social backgrounds.

¡HOLA!/HELLO!

....

....

4 Work in groups. You are the editors of one of the three magazines in Exercise 3 (decide which one). You must choose the best four stories for your readers. When you have decided, be ready to explain the reasons for your choice.

SON OF FAMOUS FILM STAR ARRESTED FOR DRUG DEALING

HOW TO COPE WITH STRESS AT WORK

SPANISH ROYAL FAMILY ON HOLIDAY IN BARBADOS

LEADING POLITICIAN REVEALS HIS SECRET FIGHT AGAINST CANCER

MERYL STREEP TALKS ABOUT DISCRIMINATION AGAINST WOMEN IN THE FILM INDUSTRY

DO WOMEN KNOW HOW TO USE MAKE-UP? We talk to the experts

NEW FACTS ABOUT HIV

CELEBRITIES GATHER TO SUPPORT CONCERT FOR CHARITY

HOW DOES THE NEW PORSCHE COMPARE WITH ITS JAPANESE RIVALS? Our test drive provided quite a few surprises!

WOMEN ARE NOT THE ONLY ONES TO SUFFER FROM SEXUAL HARASSMENT. We talk to men who feel intimidated by their female bosses.

WHAT THE RICH AND FAMOUS WEAR IN BED! We uncover the facts!

NEW DRUG TREATMENT FOR PREMATURE BABIES

THINKING OF TAKING A HOLIDAY IN INDIA? We report on the places to visit, food and customs.

PERSONAL STUDY WORKBOOK

In your Personal Study Workbook you will find more exercises to help you with your learning. For Unit 4, these include:

- an exercise on the present perfect and the past simple
- exercises on prepositions and lexical groups
- a reading passage about women and guns
- listening to actors talking about what magazines they read and why
- a questionnaire for you to complete and discuss with your speaking partner

REVIEW OF UNIT 2

1 What was that noise? vocabulary: ways of talking

Read this script from a television programme. The sound effects and directions to the actors are missing. Work with a partner and make it more dramatic by instructing the actors to speak in particular ways.

SCENE: in a bank. Several cashiers are at work, and there are two customers: a middle-aged man and a woman with two children.

CASHIER: How would you like it?
MAN: Sorry?
                                        In a loud voice
CASHIER: I said, 'How would you like it?' Tens? Fives?
MAN: Oh, tens, please.

Two robbers enter, one with a stocking over his head.

FIRST ROBBER: Right everyone, down on the floor.
CHILD: Oh, no! Help!
WOMAN: Ssh! Get down!
SECOND ROBBER: Psst, Bert – I've forgotten my stocking!
FIRST ROBBER: You fool! I can't trust you to do anything.
MAN: Oh, my God. No. Not you!
WOMAN: Do you know him?
MAN: Yes, you know him too – he works in the greengrocer's in the High Street.
CASHIER: 10, 20, 30, 40 ...
CHILD: Waaaaaaaahhhhh!
FIRST ROBBER: Be quiet! I've had enough of this. What a morning. Come on, Eric. Leave the building. Act natural. Be casual.
CUSTOMERS: Hurray!!!

Form groups. Act the scene in the way you have decided.

2 Could I have a blah blah, please? pronunciation: word stress

Work with a partner and complete the dialogues using vocabulary appropriate to the word stress indicated.

                        hospital
Example: *Have you ever worked in a O o o?*
                        clinic
        No, but I once worked in a O o.

1. A: Could I have a kilo of O o o, please?
   B: Sorry. We've run out. We've got some very nice o O o, though.
   A: No, thanks.

2. C: Do you know if there is a O o o near here?
   D: Yes, there's one over there next to the O o.

3. E: Have you ever been to o O o o?
   F: Yes. I preferred it to O o o, actually.

4. G: Do you mind if I borrow your O o?

   H: Not at all. It's over there, in my O o.

5. I: Have you got any books on o o O o?

   J: No, I'm afraid not. But I can easily find you one on O o.

Now read some of your dialogues to the class. Do they think you've chosen words with the stress indicated?

REVIEW OF UNIT 3

1 The same or the opposite? | synonyms and opposites |

Work alone. For each of the words in the box, write *either* a word or phrase with a similar meaning *or* a word or phrase with the opposite meaning.

Example: tidy ≠ *untidy*.......... hard .= *difficult* ≠ *soft*

> = similar meaning
> ≠ opposite meaning

worried ....   fabulous ....   frightened ....

complicated ....   to refuse ....   to be keen on something ....

to improve ....   to win ....   unusual ....

shy ....   boring ....   wet ....

Now work with your partner. Say one of the words you wrote down, and see if your partner can give you the correct synonym or opposite from the box.

Example: A: *Difficult.*
        B: *Hard?*
        A: *That's right.*

2 Telepathy | -ing form or infinitive |

Think about learning English in class and out of class. Then complete the sentences alone, using the correct form of a verb. Don't look at other learners' sentences, but try to write similar sentences to them. Don't repeat any sentence endings.

When I'm in class, I enjoy ....

Sometimes learners refuse ....

Before class, I spend about ten minutes ....

When I'm doing an exercise, I can't stand ....

When you are speaking English, you can't avoid ....

....

Our teacher sometimes tries to persuade us ....

....

I never worry about ....

Work in groups of about five or six. Each of you should read aloud your first sentence. How many sentences are the same or nearly the same? Count the score. Then do the same with the other sentences.

Which group had the highest number of similar sentences? Are they telepathic?

5

RELATIONSHIPS

Language focus:	Vocabulary:
revision of question forms	relationships
use of the possessive 's	verb + preposition
probability and possibility	
prepositions in *wh-* questions	

WHO WAS OONA MARRIED TO?

vocabulary; question forms; possessive 's

1 Look at the Chaplin family tree, and find the following people:

Oona O'Neill   Hannah Chaplin   Lita Grey   Sydney Earle Chaplin

What relation are they to Charlie Chaplin? Discuss with a partner.

2 🔲🔲 Now listen to the story of this remarkable group of people. Fill in the missing names on the family tree. (Several people in this family are called Charles or Sydney!) Compare your answers in groups.

3 With a partner, write down the answers to these questions:

1. Who was Oona O'Neill's father-in-law?
2. What's the name of Victoria's nephew?
3. What was the name of Charlie Chaplin's brother-in-law?
4. What are the names of Shane's cousins?
5. What are the names of Geraldine's stepbrothers?
6. Who is Geraldine's niece?
7. Who was Victoria's great-grandfather?

4 Draw a tree of your own family, or a friend's family. Leave some spaces (as in Exercise 1). Swap trees with a partner and then ask each other questions to complete the trees.

5 Write down two possible answers for each question below. Look at the example first.

Example: *Who is your nephew?*
        It could be: a. *Your brother's son.* or b. *Your sister's son.*

1. Who is your uncle?
2. Who is your great grandmother?
3. Who is your cousin?
4. Who is your brother-in-law?
5. Who is your niece?
6. Who is your stepbrother?

Discuss your answers with a partner.

6 Look at the pictures. When do we use *'s* and when do we use *s'*?

1. the child's mother
2. the boy's father
3. the boys' father
4. the students' teacher
5. the children's grandparents

POSSIBLE INFLUENCES
probability and possibility

1 Put the expressions in the diagram. Some expressions go in the same space.

It is unlikely to be true.
It may be true.
I doubt if it is true.
It is probably true.
It might be true.
It definitely isn't true.
It is likely to be true.
It is definitely true.

Compare your answers with a partner.

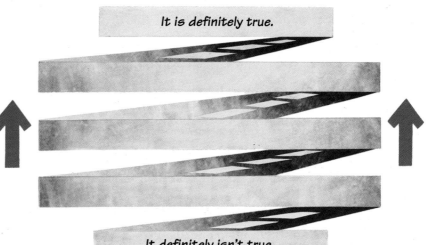

It is definitely true.

It definitely isn't true.

2 Write three sentences about yourself which are either true or false. Try to choose things which other people in your group won't know.

Examples: *I have never been in an aeroplane.*
I can speak Portuguese.
All my brothers and sisters were born in the same month.

Work in small groups. Listen to other people's sentences and say if you think they are true, using the phrases in Exercise 1. At the end, tell the group which sentences were true/false.

3 Discuss these questions in the same groups.

1. How many people in your group are …
   – the first child in their family?   – the youngest child in their family?
   – a middle child in their family?   – the only child in their family?
2. Do you like your position in your family, or would you prefer to be in a different position? If so, why?

4 Read this text about first-born and later children. (Some of the information is true, and some is not true.)

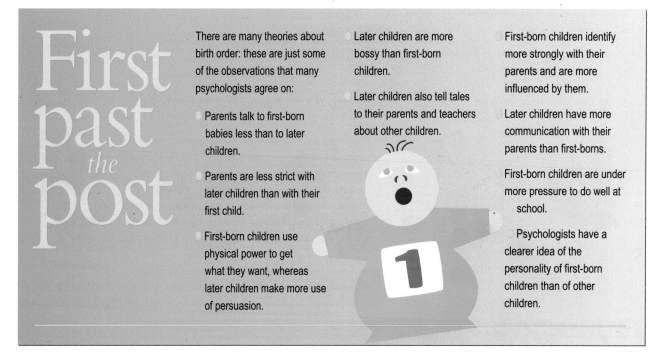

First past the post

There are many theories about birth order: these are just some of the observations that many psychologists agree on:

- Parents talk to first-born babies less than to later children.

- Parents are less strict with later children than with their first child.

- First-born children use physical power to get what they want, whereas later children make more use of persuasion.

- Later children are more bossy than first-born children.

- Later children also tell tales to their parents and teachers about other children.

- First-born children identify more strongly with their parents and are more influenced by them.

- Later children have more communication with their parents than first-borns.

- First-born children are under more pressure to do well at school.

- Psychologists have a clearer idea of the personality of first-born children than of other children.

In groups, discuss and make corrections to the nine points, using the language from Exercise 1. When you have finished, look at the corrected text on page 171.

5 Complete these sentences about other relationships.

1. .... often have a difficult relationship with teenagers.
2. .... find it easier to talk to their daughters than their sons.
3. Only children tend to communicate more easily with .... than children from large families.
4. When children ...., they get on better with their brothers and sisters.
5. Grandparents .... their grandchildren.

Give your sentences to other people in the group. Do they think your sentences are definitely true, probably true, etc.?

1 Imagine these situations. Complete the questions using the words in the box. Use a dictionary if necessary.

1. You feel stressed at work.
   Who could you talk .... ?
2. You have a personal problem.
   Who could you confide .... ?
3. You are going on an adventure holiday where you have to share a very small tent.
   Who could you spend a week .... ?
4. You have an accident at home and need urgent help.
   Who would you call .... help?
5. You have a financial problem.
   Who would you turn .... for advice?
   Who could you borrow money .... ?
6. You need help, but you don't want anyone to know.
   Who could you rely .... to keep a secret?
7. Someone asks you to make a false excuse for them.
   Who would you be prepared to lie .... ?

to	on	on	from	to	in
with	for				

2 🔲 Listen to the questions from Exercise 1 on the recording, and mark the main stress in each one.

Example: *Who could you talk to?*

What do you notice about the stress in these questions? Practise saying them, paying attention to sentence stress.

3 Work with a partner. Ask each other the questions and discuss the answers.

4 Read this text, then study the star diagrams.

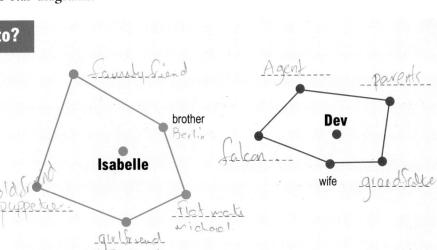

Who are you closest to?

A 'star diagram' is a map of your relationships. It shows who you are closest to. 'You' are in the centre of the diagram, and some of the people you know are placed on the paper, nearer or further away from you, depending how close their relationship is to you. So if, for example, you are very close to your sister, but less close to your brother, the diagram will demonstrate that.

🔲 Listen to the two people talking about their diagrams and fill in the missing names.

5 With a partner, talk about these questions.

1. Who is Isabelle closest to?
2. Who did she grow up with?
3. Who does she share a flat with?
4. In difficulty, who does she turn to?
5. Who is Dev closest to?
6. Who does he turn to for advice?
7. Who does he find it difficult to talk to?
8. Who does he rely on for work?

PERSONAL STUDY WORKBOOK

In your Personal Study Workbook, you will find more exercises to help you with your learning. For Unit 5, these include:

- word building and vocabulary
- practice of possibility and probability
- listening to people describing their families
- a writing activity on connecting ideas
- another page of your visual dictionary to complete – about relationships

---

REVIEW AND DEVELOPMENT

REVIEW OF UNIT 3

1 It's a kind of ball game | paraphrasing |

Add at least three words to each of the definitions.

Example: It's a kind of ball game.
 football, volleyball, squash

1. It's a type of fruit and it's yellow.
   Banana,
2. It's a thing you use for writing.

3. It's somewhere to sleep if you go away on holiday.

4. It's someone who works in a hospital.

5. It's the stuff people have on their bathroom shelf.

6. It's a kind of book.

Compare your answers with a partner.
Work with a new partner. Choose some of your words, and give clearer definitions or paraphrases of them. See if your partner can guess the words.

Example: A: It's a kind of ball game that you play on a court, there are two players …
 B: Tennis?
 A: No, they use a smaller ball and they play against a wall …
 B: Squash?
 A: That's right.

2 You need a ball but you don't need a racket   sports vocabulary

Work with a partner. Read the sentences and underline the mistake in each one. Then think of a suitable word or phrase to put in its place.

a pair of boots

Example: *For football, you need a pair of shorts and a shirt, ~~a racket~~, goalposts and a ball.*

1. For tennis, you need a racket, a pair of trainers, a saddle and a net.
2. For Monopoly, you need a dice, some toy money and a referee.
3. For fishing, you need a fishing rod, a line and a crash helmet.
4. For swimming, you need a skipping rope, a swimsuit or swimming trunks and a pair of goggles.
5. For golf, you need a pair of skates, golf clubs and a tee.
6. For an athletics meeting, you need a track, a dartboard, javelins and hurdles.

Write a list of your own, with one wrong word. Show it to others and see if they can find the mistake.

REVIEW OF UNIT 4

1 My verb, your preposition   vocabulary

Work with a partner. One of you must complete sentences 1–8 on this page, while the other completes sentences 9–16 on page 171. When you have finished, compare your sentences.

1. I can't remember who I voted .... in the last election.
2. The magazine is aimed .... women in their early twenties.
3. I just couldn't cope .... all the problems at once.
4. They have invested a lot of money .... that company.
5. We are thinking .... going to Canada for our holiday.
6. She suffers .... arthritis so she's in a lot of pain.
7. The man was arrested .... the murder of the young policewoman.
8. If you compare this film .... her last film, you can see a big difference.

2 Personal factfile   past simple vs. present perfect

Read through these sentences. Are they *true* or *false* for you?

1. I've worked in different countries.
2. I've never been to Africa.
3. I've been to the top of the Eiffel Tower.
4. I've met a famous person.
5. I've seen a ghost.
6. I've eaten snails.
7. I've worked hard this month.
8. I worked hard last month.
9. I watched a lot of television last night.
10. I've spent too much money this week.

Interview other people in the class, like this:

A: *Have you ever worked in different countries?*
B: *No, never.*
A: *OK, well, have you met anyone famous?*
B: *Yes, I have.*
A: *Who?*
B: *I won a competition, and the first prize was dinner with Michelle Pfeiffer.*

6

LIFE'S LITTLE CHORES

Language focus:	Vocabulary:
past continuous	phrasal verbs
reflexive pronouns	verb prefix *un-*
get + past participle	accidents and injuries
functional language	

TURNING ON AND TURNING OFF
opposites; phrasal verbs; verb prefix un-

1 Work with a partner. Write down what the person is doing in each of these pictures. If necessary, look at the list of verbs on page 171.

Example: *Picture 1. A man is turning a light on.*

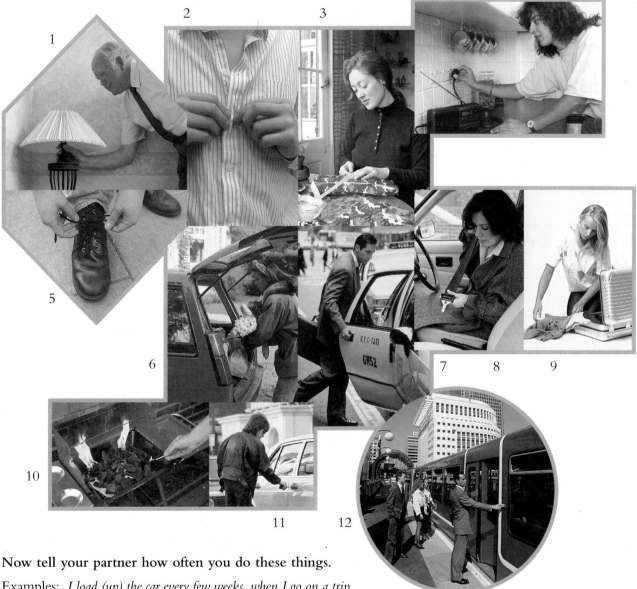

Now tell your partner how often you do these things.

Examples: *I load (up) the car every few weeks, when I go on a trip.*
            I rarely get on trains.

2 With your partner, think of another noun you could use with each of the verbs. (Some learners' dictionaries will help you.)

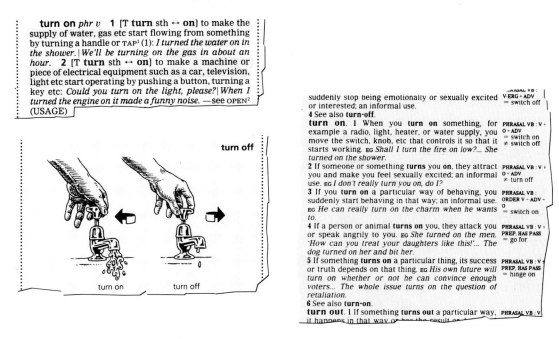

turn on *phr v* **1** [T **turn** sth ↔ **on**] to make the supply of water, gas etc start flowing from something by turning a handle or TAP¹ (1): *I turned the water on in the shower.* | *We'll be turning on the gas in about an hour.* **2** [T **turn** sth ↔ **on**] to make a machine or piece of electrical equipment such as a car, television, light etc start operating by pushing a button, turning a key etc: *Could you turn on the light, please?* | *When I turned the engine on it made a funny noise.* —see OPEN² (USAGE)

turn off

turn on   turn off

suddenly stop being emotionally or sexually excited or interested; an informal use.
4 See also **turn-off**.
turn on. **1** When you **turn on** something, for example a radio, light, heater, or water supply, you move the switch, knob, etc that controls it so that it starts working. EG *Shall I turn the fire on low?... She turned on the shower.*
2 If someone or something **turns** you **on**, they attract you and make you feel sexually excited; an informal use. EG *I don't really turn you on, do I?*
3 If you **turn on** a particular way of behaving, you suddenly start behaving in that way; an informal use. EG *He can really turn on the charm when he wants to.*
4 If a person or animal **turns on** you, they attack you or speak angrily to you. EG *She turned on the men. 'How can you treat your daughters like this!'... The dog turned on her and bit her.*
5 If something **turns on** a particular thing, its success or truth depends on that thing. EG *His own future will turn on whether or not he can convince enough voters... The whole issue turns on the question of retaliation.*
6 See also **turn-on**.
turn out. **1** If something **turns out** a particular way, it happens in that way ...

...RASAL VB :
V·ERG + ADV
= switch off

PHRASAL VB : V +
O + ADV
= switch on
≠ switch off

PHRASAL VB : V +
O + ADV
≠ turn off

PHRASAL VB :
ORDER V - ADV -
O
= switch on

PHRASAL VB : V +
PREP. HAS PASS
= go for

PHRASAL VB : V +
PREP. HAS PASS
= hinge on

PHRASAL VB : V

Example: *You can turn on a **radio** or a **light** or a **shower**.*

Compare your answers in small groups.

3 The phrasal verbs in pictures 1–6 are all *separable*. Read the grammar explanation below.

> If the object is a noun, you can put it before or after the particle:
> *He's turning **the light** on.*
> *He's turning on **the light**.*
> If the object is a pronoun, it must go between the verb and the particle:
> *He's turning **it** on.*
> not ~~He's turning on it.~~

Make sentences about pictures 1–6 again, using the pronoun *it* or *them*.

4 Write the opposite of each verb in the 12 sentences you wrote in Exercise 1. Some require the prefix *un-* (e.g. *pack – unpack*); others require a phrasal verb (e.g. *turn on – turn off*). Check whether the new phrasal verbs are separable.
When you've finished, test your partner, like this:

B: *When do you turn off a light?*
A: *When you go out of the room.*
A: *When do you unpack a suitcase?*
B: *When you get to your destination.*

5 ▭▭ Listen to the recording and decide which actions from Exercise 1 are being described. Compare your answers with a partner.

6 Work with the same partner. Write a paragraph like the ones you heard in Exercise 5 about another everyday activity of your choice. Try not to use words which will make it too easy to guess the action.

Give your paragraph to another pair. Can they guess what you are describing?

1 Match the situations on the left with the possible consequences on the right. Use a dictionary if necessary.

1. making a hot drink
2. plugging something in
3. crossing a busy road
4. walking home late at night
5. getting out of the shower
6. lighting a fire
7. taking a friend's dog for a walk

a. you can get an electric shock
b. you can burn yourself
c. you can slip over and hurt yourself
d. you can spill it and scald yourself
e. you can get bitten
f. you can get mugged
g. you can get knocked down

2 What is the difference between these two sentences?

1. He bit himself.   2. He got bitten.

Check your answers in the Grammar Reference on page 162 and read about the use of reflexive pronouns and *get* + past participle.

With your partner, think of two more examples of each of these constructions.

3 Read what happened in one of the situations above and answer the questions below.

The other day I was taking my brother's dog for a walk by the river. Suddenly it jumped in, and I slipped over and fell in. When I got to my feet, the dog was on the bank with a surprised look on its face.

1. What tense is used in the first sentence?
2. Why is the verb in the first sentence in a different tense from all the others in the story?

4 Correct any tense mistakes in this story and compare with a partner.

> I decided to go out with some friends for dinner last week. We were having a lovely time. When I walked home late at night, a frightening-looking man came up to me and asked me what time it was. This made me very nervous, but I was telling him and he thanked me and walked away. The next day, I saw his picture in my local newspaper. The police wanted to interview him about the murder of his business partner the previous evening.

5 Look at the situations in Exercise 1. Think of something that happened to you, or invent something based on one of those situations.
Tell your stories in small groups. Whose stories are true, and whose are invented?

DO YOU QUEUE?

1 Discuss your answers to these questions with a partner.

1. How many times a day do you have to queue for things? What do you have to queue for?
2. Do you consider yourself to be a patient person?
3. How long would you be prepared to queue for the following?
   - to use a public phone box
   - to buy bread at the best bakery in town
   - to get tickets for your all-time favourite singer/musician/group/orchestra
   - to obtain a visa for a country you are very keen to visit
   - to see a doctor about back pain
   - to collect a free English–English dictionary
4. Is it acceptable to jump a queue? If so, in what circumstances?
5. Have you ever been abroad and had to queue for something which you would not queue for at home?

Now think of two different questions to ask about queuing, and ask them in small groups.

2 Read the text about queuing and underline five things you didn't know before you started reading.

Have we queued our last?

In 1837, the historian Carlyle made the first recorded use of the word 'queue'. He spoke of the French and their 'talent of spontaneously standing in a queue'. Forty years later Paris was still the best place to wait in line.

However, queuing became popular in Britain too. The Second World War was the golden age of queuing, and people joined any line in the hope that it was a queue for something to buy. This was the source of many Second World War jokes:
Shopkeeper to customer: Excuse me, miss, are you pregnant?
Young woman: Well, I wasn't when I joined the queue.

Today, according to research in America, we (in Britain) can spend up to 5 years of our lives queuing – as opposed to twelve months looking for things we have lost. But things may be changing. Many people no longer have the patience to stand in a queue. The law of the jungle has begun to operate at bus stops, with people using their elbows to push others out of the way. Dr David Worthington, an expert in queuing, believes this trend may continue, 'As we get more Europeanised, that may be a tendency.'

One way to make life easier is to introduce 'queue management'. Customers at supermarket cheese counters can now take a ticket with a number which appears on a screen when it is their turn. And while they wait for their number they can do a bit of shopping.
In some booking offices there is also a system telling customers how long they may have to wait before they are served.

One of the latest technical innovations is an electronic scanner which can read all the contents of your shopping trolley in just a few seconds. If these become popular, queuing in supermarkets may become a thing of the past.

But some people just like queuing. One man queued all night for Harrods famous January sale, and then returned home for breakfast at nine o'clock the next morning without going into the shop.

Work in small groups and shut your books before you begin this exercise. Take turns to say a fact you learnt from the text. Count the number of facts the group has learnt, then compare your scores with other groups.

3 Work in small groups and decide what you would say or do in these situations in queues. (You might decide to do nothing.)

1. You are in the middle of a crowded compartment on a train and you want to get off at the next stop. What could you say to the people in front of you?
2. You want to join a queue in a market to buy vegetables, but you are not sure where the queue ends. What would you do or say?
3. You are in a queue waiting to pay at the supermarket. You suddenly remember you have forgotten to buy something. You don't want to lose your place. What could you say to the person behind you?
4. You are in a long queue and someone tries to push in in front of you. What would you do or say?
5. You have to catch a train which is leaving in a couple of minutes, and the queue you are in at the ticket office is moving very slowly. What would you do or say?

4 🎧 Listen to the recording. Write down what the speakers say in each situation if it is different from what you discussed.

Discuss the following in small groups.

1. What is your opinion of what the speakers say?
2. Do they use any phrases which would be useful in other situations? If so, which?

PERSONAL STUDY WORKBOOK

In your Personal Study Workbook, you will find more exercises to help you with your learning. For Unit 6, these include:

- an exercise on the past simple and past continuous
- a vocabulary exercise on words that go together
- practice of reflexive pronouns and *get* + past participle
- listening and guessing what people are talking about
- a letter to read and write

REVIEW AND DEVELOPMENT

REVIEW OF UNIT 4

1 Magazine titles | speaking |

Look at the following magazine titles. What do you think each one is about? Compare with a partner.

Just Desserts	Profit & Loss	DIY
Stage	Kick Start	Take-off
In the Saddle	Melody Maker	Taste
Scissors	Serve and Volley	Making Waves
Goal	On the Slopes	What's On

Example: Just Desserts *is a cookery magazine.*

2 How do you say the letter *o*? | pronunciation |

Put the words in the correct column, according to the pronunciation of the letter *o*.

/ʌ/	/əʊ/	/ə/	/uː/
some	*home*	*complain*	*who*
....	....	....	....
....	....	....	....
....	....	....	....
....	....	....	....

company   editor   scoop   hello   famous   compare   courage
through   radio   lose   social   son   other   too   section   cope

🎧 Listen to the recording to check your answers.

---

3 Correct the mistakes | present perfect with *for, since* and *yet* |

Find the mistakes and correct them. Not all the sentences are incorrect, so be careful.

1. I haven't seen them since three weeks.
2. Did you finish it yet?
3. I've been here since half past nine.
4. I haven't received yet the letters.
5. They've lived there for more than ten years.
6. Since I've been fourteen I haven't bought any CDs.
7. That chair broke weeks ago and nobody has repaired it yet.
8. I don't eat meat since ten years.

REVIEW OF UNIT 5

1 A sad tale | verb + preposition |

Complete the story with the correct prepositions, then compare with a partner.

John Riley's story is not unique. After leaving home, he moved into a flat with two young men from work. He didn't know either of them very well, but they both had good jobs and earned a lot more than him. John spent a lot of time .... them, but found that he couldn't keep up with their expensive lifestyle. So, first he borrowed money .... friends, but soon he had to lie .... his parents in order to get larger sums of money. Then he started to get letters from his bank manager who wanted to talk .... him about his debts.

Worried that his parents might find out, he decided to turn .... his uncle who he relied .... and who he had always been close .... as a child. He was lucky – his uncle paid his debts, but more important, taught him about organising his money wisely.

Confiding .... his uncle was the best thing he ever did, for he went on to become a financial adviser – clearly, a man who had learnt .... his experiences.

2 Elephants cannot jump | possibility and probability |

Work in small groups. Discuss the statements, using these expressions.

That's likely to be true.
That's unlikely to be true.
That's definitely not true.
That's definitely true.
That may/might be true.
I doubt if that's true.

1. Elephants cannot jump.
2. Six different languages are spoken in India.
3. Typewriters were first developed to help the blind.
4. A gorilla's brain weighs 5 kg.
5. The word *school* comes from the Greek word *skhole* meaning leisure.
6. In Italy, tulips are grown partly because they are beautiful, but also because they are eaten as part of a salad.
7. The yo-yo was originally used in the Philippines as a jungle weapon.
8. During their studies, medical students increase their vocabulary by 10,000 words.

COURSES

Language focus: uncountable nouns ending in *s* defining relative clauses (1) adjective + infinitive *ask/tell* + object + infinitive obligation in the past	Vocabulary: education subjects, courses and exams household activities

TURNING POINTS vocabulary: education; relative clauses

1 Work with a partner and check that you understand and can pronounce these words.

maths   psychology   chemistry   philosophy   art   religion   politics
history   agriculture   medicine   economics   aerobics   engineering   physics
literature   electronics   statistics   athletics   architecture   computer studies

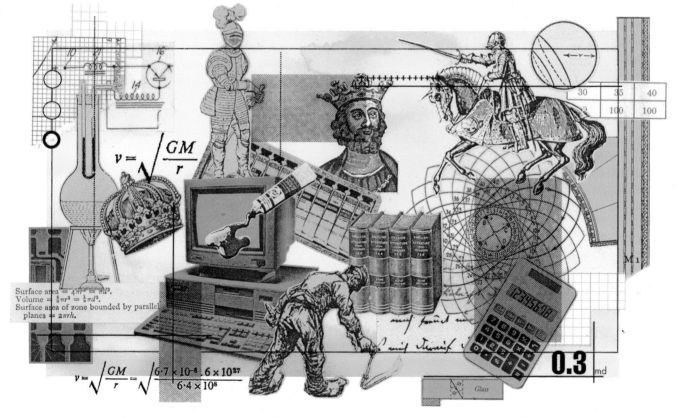

In your country, do people do these subjects at school, at university or not at all? Discuss in groups.

2 Underline the words above which end in *s*. They look plural, but in fact they are uncountable, so they take a singular verb.

Example: *Maths **was** my favourite subject at school.*

Is it the same in your language? Tell a partner.

TURNING POINTS

47

3 Fill the gaps with words from the list below.

1. You can do, sit, ..., pass or .... an exam.
2. You can get a degree, a diploma or a ....
3. You can be hopeless at, ... at, good at or .... at a subject.
4. You can do well or .... in a subject.
5. You can register for or .... on a course.

> certificate   badly   take   brilliant   enrol   bad   fail

In small groups, talk about your experiences. Use the vocabulary above and words from Exercise 1.

Examples: *The last time I sat an exam was five years ago, and fortunately I passed it. It was the last exam in a management course.*
I was quite good at arts subjects at school, but hopeless at maths.

4 ⬛ Listen to a woman describing a turning point in her education. Make notes on the following:

1. When did it happen?   2. What was the turning point?   3. What happened as a result?

5 Look at these examples:

1. *The thing **that** changed my life was university.*
2. *The thing **(that)** I hated most was chemistry.*

In 1, you have to include *that*, but in 2, you can leave it out. Why? (Think about the number of subjects in each sentence.) Discuss with a partner.

6 Can you leave out *that* in the first six sentences? What about *who* in the seventh sentence?

1. The last course that I did was ....
2. The thing that interested me most at school was ....
3. The subject that I knew most about was ....
4. The subject that I knew least about was ....
5. The biggest problem that I had at college was ....
6. The biggest problem that I had at school was ....
7. The person who inspired me most was ....

Complete the sentences about your own education, then discuss them in small groups.

NOT EASY TO BE A BUTLER   adjective + infinitive; *ask/tell* + object + infinitive

1 Imagine you were thinking of becoming a butler. Complete these sentences, then compare your ideas in groups.

Example: *I would have the opportunity to* meet people and to travel with my employer.

1. I might find it difficult to ....
2. It would be interesting to ....
3. I might find it boring to ....
4. I would be able to ....
5. It would be horrible to ....
6. I wouldn't be willing to ....

2 Look at the pictures. Which duties would a trainee butler have to learn? Which are the easiest or most difficult to learn? Discuss in small groups.

3 Ivor Spencer runs a training course for people who want to be butlers. Read the text, and find out:

1. what skills are learnt   2. how the job has changed

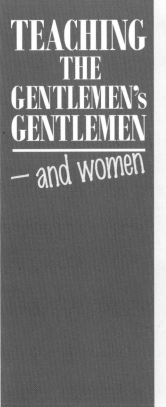

TEACHING THE GENTLEMEN's GENTLEMEN
– and women

Have you ever wondered what it would be like to train to be a butler? If so, you could stop wondering and find out for yourself by doing Ivor Spencer's special course for trainee butlers. It costs just over £3,000, but that includes 86 lessons on a wide range of skills: how to bow, iron the morning newspaper, present and pour wine, pack a suitcase and quietly remove a drunken party guest. Students announce imaginary visitors, and walk with wine glasses on their heads while carrying a magnum of champagne on a tray.

Most of the butlers-to-be are in their early twenties and a few of them are women. Previous occupations are irrelevant; past courses have included a former British colonel and an American tax official. Employers in the past were royalty, but today most are businessmen, and butlers generally prefer to work in the United States because American employers are the most friendly and generous.

'What we look for is perfection,' the impeccably-dressed Spencer says. This explains the quick quiz questions. 'James, what is a butler's attitude towards his employer?'
'Friendly, but never familiar, sir.'
'Very good. Martin, tell me about a butler's personal hygiene.'
'Bath or shower twice a day, brush teeth at least four times a day, and never eat onions, curry or garlic, even on days off.'
'That is correct.'

Traditionally, a butler's duties were to polish silver, serve food and drinks and generally supervise the other staff employed in the house. Some of those things are still true, but nowadays a butler is really much more a 'manager'. He may have to run three or four houses, handle the accounts of the staff – and that may include the crew of the yacht and the helicopter – and handle all the travel arrangements for his employer.

4 How *should* a butler 'quietly remove a drunken party guest'? Discuss with a partner and then exchange your ideas with another pair. You may need to use these structures:

to ask
to tell   someone (not) to do something
to explain that (something ...)
to apologise for (something)

5 🔊 Listen to an interview with a trainee butler and complete these sentences.

1. The host will tell the butler ....
2. The butler will tell another servant ....
3. The butler will ask the guest ....
4. The butler will apologise ....
5. The butler will explain ....
6. He will ask the guest ....
7. He will also ask the guest ....
8. The butler will then order ....

6 Work in small groups. What would you ask or tell a butler to do for you, if you had one?

Examples: *We would ask a butler to look up English words in a dictionary for us.*
We would tell the butler not to disturb us until ten o'clock in the morning.

Tell your ideas to the rest of the class.

AN ACTOR'S LIFE FOR ME   vocabulary: personal qualities; obligation in the past

1 Which actors and actresses do you admire most? Why? Which are their greatest roles? Discuss in small groups.

2 Read this text about an actor's skills and do the task below.

Can acting be taught?

You cannot teach someone to be 'talented', but if an actor possesses natural talent, they must still learn 5 how to express it through the skills of the performer: command of voice and speech; a feeling for words, movement and body 10 language; and how to bring all these things together.

Voice and speech is the actor's primary skill. Most of their communication is 15 through the spoken word, and the scripts actors work with now require a greater variety of voices and accents than they did in the 20 past. However, as the actor is also the interpreter of the text, he or she must be very responsive to the character's use of 25 language.

Present-day acting is also very visual and makes great demands on the actor in terms of physical 30 movement. The actor may have to represent not only many types of people but also objects and machines. Repose and expressiveness 35 are qualities actors need to convey through the body. They may even find themselves working in performances which 40 involve dancing, falling and acrobatics.

Mental training is vital too. Actors have to give 100% attention to what 45 they are doing; they have to think and respond creatively; to look and learn; and recall and recreate emotion in a 50 selective way. They also have to think deeply about a text and analyse it. Finally, actors have to learn to work with each other, 55 the director and the audience.

Acting is a very practical business, and what you do has to look and sound 60 right. The audience may not know about the mysteries of acting but they do know about people and life.

Is it true that actors may have to be …
– good mimics?
– fit?
– agile?
– observant?
– sensitive?

Find phrases or lines in the text to justify your answers, and then compare with a partner.

3 Work in small groups and choose two of the jobs below. Which of the qualities in Exercise 2 (both the text and the questions) do these people have to have? Remember: *don't have to = it's not necessary.*

Example: *ballet dancers*
      They have to be agile.
      They might have to be creative.
      They don't have to be good mimics.

politicians   long distance lorry drivers
violinists in an orchestra   interpreters
writers   cartoonists

4 ▭▭ ▭▭ Listen to two actors talking about their drama training. Make notes on what they had to do and didn't have to do.

5 What about you? Which of the qualities in Exercise 3 are important to you in your personal or professional life? Tell your partner.

PERSONAL STUDY WORKBOOK

In your Personal Study Workbook, you will find more exercises to help you with your learning. In Unit 6, these include:

- reading and listening texts about different educational courses
- a listen and answer exercise to test vocabulary
- a grammar exercise on sentence construction
- guided writing
- another page of your visual dictionary to complete – about education

---

REVIEW AND DEVELOPMENT

REVIEW OF UNIT 5

1 Changing family patterns   possibility and probability

A Discuss these questions with a partner, then compare your opinions with others in the class.

1. How important is the family unit in your society now?
2. Is it becoming more important or less important?
3. Are more children living with single parents?
4. What is the situation likely to be ten years from now?

B Now read these predictions about family patterns in Europe.

FAMILIES COULD BECOME IRRELEVANT

According to a report published recently, society in Europe will become increasingly 'matrilineal', with more and more children brought up solely by their mothers.

The trend will be for families to come under greater stress, with children being much more ready to divorce their parents. As a result, the survey predicts that a greater proportion of children will be brought up by mothers alone.

If this trend continues, the only permanent and lasting relationship will be between mothers and their children.

The report suggests that children brought up by one parent might suffer harmful effects in terms of education, economic prospects, health and psychological stress. In terms of creating a better environment for children, they say, two parents are better than one.

With a partner, make a list of the predictions in the article under the following three headings.

According to the article, what things:

   may happen?   *are likely to happen?*   *will definitely happen?*

Compare your list with others. Do you agree with the article?

2 How good is your memory? vocabulary

Work in groups. Make a list of all the possible family relationships. Don't stop until you have at least twenty! Look again at the first lesson in Unit 5 if you need help.

Examples: *brother   sister-in-law*

REVIEW OF UNIT 6

1 Consequences past continuous

Here are the results of different actions. What do you think the person was doing in each case? Write down a logical answer and then compare in groups.

Example: *He cut his finger.*
Perhaps he was preparing the dinner.

1. She slipped on a piece of soap.
2. He laughed out loud.
3. He burnt himself.
4. She cut her foot on the rocks.
5. He fell asleep and crashed into a tree.
6. The teacher asked them to be quiet.
7. She fell off.
8. He spilt it all over the floor.

2 When did you last ...? phrasal verbs

Work in small groups. Tell each other when you last did these things, and say what you did.

Example: *take something off*
I took something off twenty minutes ago. I was hot, so I took my jacket off.

When did you last ...
– get into something moving?
– put something out?
– turn something off?
– plug something in?
– get off something?
– do something up?
– throw something away?
– push in somewhere?
– take something off?
– fall over something?

Think of two more phrasal verbs like these, then ask your group about them.

Example: *When did you last try something on?*

8

ALL IN A DAY'S WORK

Language focus:	Vocabulary:
link words: concession and addition	work vocabulary
functional language: making and refusing requests,	verb + noun collocations
asking for and refusing permission	fixed phrases

HOW DO YOU COPE? functional language

1 When was the last time you had to do any of the following things, either at work or at home?

What was the situation, and how easy or difficult did you find it?

- ask someone to do something they didn't want to do
- get some information over the phone
- give someone some bad news
- ask someone for permission to do something
- refuse someone permission to do something

Compare your answers in small groups.
Who had the most difficult situation?

2 Work with a partner. Which phrases in the speech bubbles could you use in the situations in Exercise 1?

Note: These phrases are often used either in more formal situations, or in situations where the speaker needs to be careful about how they say something.

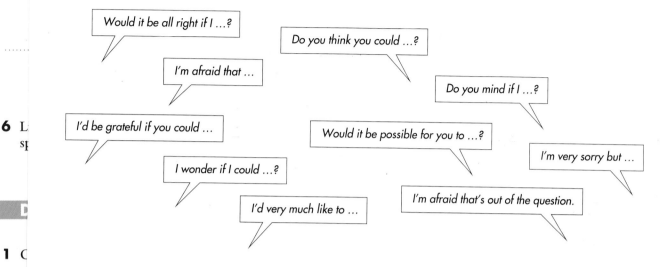

Would it be all right if I ...?

Do you think you could ...?

I'm afraid that ...

Do you mind if I ...?

I'd be grateful if you could ...

Would it be possible for you to ...?

I'm very sorry but ...

I wonder if I could ...?

I'd very much like to ...

I'm afraid that's out of the question.

3 Make sure you understand the situations in the boxes.

1.

You are the head of a department which is very busy at the moment. One of the people in your department asks you if they can have the day off tomorrow to go to a parents' meeting at their son's school. What do you say?

2.

You work for a multinational company and you are very keen to do a one-week course at company headquarters in Stockholm. The company has recently made a lot of cutbacks in the training budget. What do you say to your boss?

3.

Last week, you had a rather unpleasant meeting with a manager in another department. You know that there are a few questions you still need to discuss, and you imagine that the manager will not want to speak to you. Ring him/her up, and try to make an appointment.

4.

You need to get some financial information very urgently from a colleague, but it is now the end of the working day and your colleague is leaving in a few minutes. You need the information to prepare for a meeting tomorrow. What do you say?

📖 Listen to the two dialogues on the recording and answer these questions.

1. Which situation were they talking about?
2. Which phrases did you hear from Exercise 2?
3. Which dialogue do you think is more effective, and why?

4 Choose two of the remaining situations, and act them out with a partner. Use some of the language in Exercise 2.

When you have finished, act your conversations for another pair or for the class. Do they sound realistic?

3 Read the two problem situations. Which management style (1–5) is the best one to deal with the situation in each case? Discuss in small groups.

1 Every year this company closes its factory for one month during the summer and all the workers take their holiday at the same time. The manager believes the company will be more profitable if the factory stays open throughout the year. For this reason, she would like the workers to go on holiday at different times of the year.

2 In this company, the manager of a sales team has a group meeting with the other five members once a month. Apart from this they work alone, as they work in different geographical regions. The manager himself was an area sales representative in the past and knows the job well. Now he is looking for a new sales representative for a new area, and has received some job applications. Next week he is meeting the team and is wondering how much he should involve the others in the choice of the new sales representative.

4 This unit has included a lot of new vocabulary related to work. Go back over the lessons with a partner, and write down any useful new words and phrases.

PERSONAL STUDY WORKBOOK

In your Personal Study Workbook, you will find more exercises to help you with your learning. For Unit 8, these include:

- vocabulary exercises on fixed phrases and on the topic of work
- exercises on requesting and giving permission
- a text about a way of helping people through difficulties
- reading and writing memos
- a speaking partners creative thinking exercise

REVIEW AND DEVELOPMENT

REVIEW OF UNIT 6

1 How did you do it? | reflexive pronouns; *get* + past participle |

Complete the sentences in a way which demonstrates the meaning of the words.

Example: *I burnt myself*   when I was taking something out of the oven.
   when I was trying to put the fire out.

I got bitten ....
They injured themselves ....
He scalded himself ....
They got knocked down ....

2 Work with a partner. Which phrases in the speech bubbles could you use in the situations in Exercise 1?

> *Note:* These phrases are often used either in more formal situations, or in situations where the speaker needs to be careful about how they say something.

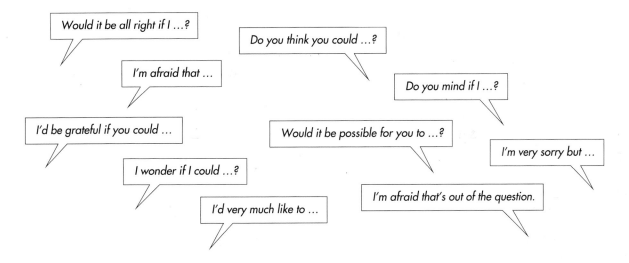

Would it be all right if I ...?

Do you think you could ...?

I'm afraid that ...

Do you mind if I ...?

I'd be grateful if you could ...

Would it be possible for you to ...?

I'm very sorry but ...

I wonder if I could ...?

I'd very much like to ...

I'm afraid that's out of the question.

3 Make sure you understand the situations in the boxes.

1.

You are the head of a department which is very busy at the moment. One of the people in your department asks you if they can have the day off tomorrow to go to a parents' meeting at their son's school. What do you say?

2.

You work for a multinational company and you are very keen to do a one-week course at company headquarters in Stockholm. The company has recently made a lot of cutbacks in the training budget. What do you say to your boss?

3.

Last week, you had a rather unpleasant meeting with a manager in another department. You know that there are a few questions you still need to discuss, and you imagine that the manager will not want to speak to you. Ring him/her up, and try to make an appointment.

4.

You need to get some financial information very urgently from a colleague, but it is now the end of the working day and your colleague is leaving in a few minutes. You need the information to prepare for a meeting tomorrow. What do you say?

📼 Listen to the two dialogues on the recording and answer these questions.

1. Which situation were they talking about?
2. Which phrases did you hear from Exercise 2?
3. Which dialogue do you think is more effective, and why?

4 Choose two of the remaining situations, and act them out with a partner. Use some of the language in Exercise 2.

When you have finished, act your conversations for another pair or for the class. Do they sound realistic?

1 Choose a word from the box to complete each of these phrases.

theory and ....   advantages and ....

pros and ....   for and ....

ups and ....

> disadvantages   practice   cons   against   downs

What do these phrases have in common?

2 Discuss these questions in small groups.

1. If you work, do you work for yourself (self-employed) or do you work for someone else (a company, an institution, etc.)? Which do you think is better, and why?
2. If you don't work, would you prefer to be self-employed or to work for someone else? Why?
3. Which jobs are usually done by people who are self-employed?

3 Read the statements about being self-employed, and check any words you don't know. Write them out in two lists: *Pros* and *Cons*.

You don't receive sickness pay.
You have more choice about the work you do.
You don't have paid holidays.
Nobody above you gives you orders.
You have nobody to share your problems with.
You have to manage your own financial affairs.
You can organise your working hours to suit yourself.
You can be flexible about holidays and days off.
You lack job security.
There is no limit to what you can do.

Discuss your answers in groups. Then add to your lists any more ideas you had in Exercise 2.

4 Work alone and link some of the most important ideas in a paragraph, using the language in the box.

One of the main advantages of being self-employed *is that* ....
....   PROS
In addition, ...

On the other hand, ...
....   CONS
Another disadvantage is that ....
....

Compare in groups. Do you all think the same things are important?

5 What are the pros and cons of working for a large, international company, compared with being self-employed? In small groups, complete the diagrams below.

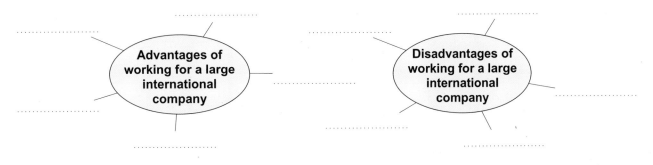

6 Link your ideas together in a paragraph, as in Exercise 4. If you prefer, prepare a short speech to give to the class on the subject, again using the link words in Exercise 4.

DEMOCRATS AND AUTOCRATS

1 Complete these sentences with verbs from the box. Compare with a partner.

1. It's the manager's job to ...*solve*........... problems.
2. Some managers .... problems with others.
3. They have to .... difficult decisions.
4. They often need to .... information first.
5. Good managers have to .... difficult situations carefully.
6. Some managers .... other people before making decisions.
7. Everyone has to .... an agreement.

make   reach   share   get   evaluate   solve   consult

2 Read the descriptions of the five different types of manager. Put the numbers 1–5 on the line, then compare in small groups. Do you know managers like these?

DEMOCRATIC MANAGER ———————————————— AUTOCRATIC MANAGER

1. You discuss problems with others as a group, and collect their ideas and suggestions. Then you make the decision alone. Others may or may not agree with you.
2. You solve the problem or make the decision alone, using information that you are able to get yourself.
3. You get information from others, and then decide on the solution alone. You may or may not tell others why you want the information.
4. You share the problem with others as a group. You all evaluate the situation and reach an agreement together. You accept the group's decision, even if it isn't your own solution.
5. You share the problem with others individually, but you do not consult them as a group. You then make the decision alone. Others may or may not agree with you.

3 Read the two problem situations. Which management style (1–5) is the best one to deal with the situation in each case? Discuss in small groups.

1 Every year this company closes its factory for one month during the summer and all the workers take their holiday at the same time. The manager believes the company will be more profitable if the factory stays open throughout the year. For this reason, she would like the workers to go on holiday at different times of the year.

2 In this company, the manager of a sales team has a group meeting with the other five members once a month. Apart from this they work alone, as they work in different geographical regions. The manager himself was an area sales representative in the past and knows the job well. Now he is looking for a new sales representative for a new area, and has received some job applications. Next week he is meeting the team and is wondering how much he should involve the others in the choice of the new sales representative.

4 This unit has included a lot of new vocabulary related to work. Go back over the lessons with a partner, and write down any useful new words and phrases.

PERSONAL STUDY WORKBOOK

In your Personal Study Workbook, you will find more exercises to help you with your learning. For Unit 8, these include:

- vocabulary exercises on fixed phrases and on the topic of work
- exercises on requesting and giving permission
- a text about a way of helping people through difficulties
- reading and writing memos
- a speaking partners creative thinking exercise

REVIEW AND DEVELOPMENT

REVIEW OF UNIT 6

1 How did you do it?   reflexive pronouns; *get* + past participle

Complete the sentences in a way which demonstrates the meaning of the words.

Example: *I burnt myself* .....*when I was taking something out of the oven.*.....
.....*when I was trying to put the fire out.*.....

I got bitten ....
They injured themselves ....
He scalded himself ....
They got knocked down ....

I cut myself ....

He got mugged ....

She hurt herself ....

I got stung ....

Now work in small groups. Are your sentences similar or different?

2 Word game   vocabulary

Do this exercise in small groups. Each person in turn must choose two words from the box which are connected in some way, and explain how.

Examples: *unlock and car: You can unlock a car door.*
elbow and push: Some people use their elbows to push in a queue.

The group must decide if each answer is acceptable. Continue until you cannot think of any more connections and all the words have been used at least once.

unlock	jump	office	queue	belt	booking	scald	push
elbow	get out of	car	turn on	shower	plug in	do up	bath
gadget	buttons	parcel	put out	wrap	unfasten	load (up)	
spill	cigar	a drink	shoelaces	tie (up)			

REVIEW OF UNIT 7

1 Spot the mistakes   grammar revision

Correct the grammar mistakes in these sentences.

1. When I was a child I did very bad at English.
2. At school we hadn't to wear a uniform.
3. The person who he inspired me most was my art teacher.
4. I apologised my mistake.
5. The examiner asked me that I read a text aloud in my oral interview.
6. Another student explained me the rule.
7. Someone told me not use the front door.
8. At university we didn't had to go to lectures every day.

Compare your answers in small groups.

2 Interested in maths?   pronunciation and word building

Complete the columns with a partner, then use a dictionary to check the word stress and the meaning of any words you don't know.

Subject	Person	Subject	Person
mathematics	mathematician	chemistry	....
politics	....	philosophy	....
athletics	....	history	....
economics	....	physics	....
engineering	....	interpreting	....

🎧 Check your answers on the recording, then practise saying the words with the correct stress.

9

FROM THE CRADLE TO THE GRAVE

Language focus:	Vocabulary:
obligation, prohibition, permission	ages and stages in life
present simple passive	birth, marriage and death
	wedding customs
	race, nationality, religion

AGES AND STAGES

1 Work with a partner and check that you understand the words in the table, then complete it using the words in the box below.

	Status	Stage
	a baby	....
	a child	childhood
	an adolescent	adolescence ....
	an adult	in your (early) 20s, 30s (mid) (late) ....
	....	retirement / when you are retired in old age

a teenager   infancy   in your teens   a pensioner   middle-aged
a kid (informal)   an elderly person

2 Tell your partner about members of your family, using any words from Exercise 1.

Example: *I've got two brothers; one is a teenager and the other is in his early twenties.*

3 Check that you understand and can pronounce the words below.

> take up gardening   have a baby   start a new career
> plan how to spend your retirement   get some qualifications   settle down
> live abroad   read serious literature   take out a pension
> appreciate good food   get married   learn about your family history

When is the best time to do each of these? Be prepared to give reasons.

Examples: *I think the best time to take up gardening is when you're middle-aged, because you are more interested in home life at that age and you need the exercise.*

or *I think the best time to take up gardening is in your teens, because it helps you to appreciate the simple and beautiful things in life.*

Discuss your answers in small groups.

4 ⊂⊃ You are going to hear three people at different stages in their lives. They are going to talk about what is most important to them, or what concerns people of their age. Before you listen, discuss with a partner what you think each person in the table might say.

	Stage	*Their main concerns*
1. David (20)	....	....
2. Judy (40s)	....	....
3. Walter (60s)	....	....

Listen and make notes on what they say.

5 Work in groups. Talk about people in your country at your stage of life. What concerns them?

At my age,   the main concern(s) is/are ....
             people are concerned about ....

RITES OF PASSAGE: THE FACTS   obligation, prohibition, permission

1 The words in *italics* are often used when people talk about aspects of birth, marriage and death. Answer the questions with a partner, using a dictionary if necessary.

1. If you *register a birth* what do you do?
2. What is the most common age for *baptism*?
3. What happens in a *registry office*?
4. In a *wedding ceremony*, who are the *bride and groom*?
5. Who are the bride's *relatives*?
6. Why do people *make a will*?
7. Where do *funerals* usually take place?
8. How is *burial* different from *cremation*?

2 Here are some facts about life in England and Wales. Are they different in your country?

Example: You can't get married under the age of 16.
In my country it's the same.
or *I don't know if it's the same or not in my country.*
or *In my country you can't get married until you are 18.*

1. You are obliged to register the birth of a baby within six weeks.

....

2. At a baptism (or similar early rites ceremony), close friends or relatives are supposed to give the child presents.

....

3. Parents don't have to send their children to school if they can provide them with a suitable education.

....

4. You are not allowed to drive a car until you are 17.

....

5. You have to get married in an authorised place. You are not allowed to get married wherever you want.

....

6. Married women are not obliged to take their husband's surname, but they can if they wish.

....

7. Traditionally the bride's father was expected to pay for his daughter's wedding, but nowadays things are changing.

....

8. You cannot be married to more than one person at the same time.

....

9. When someone in your family dies, you are allowed to have them buried or cremated.

....

10. You don't have to make a will, but it is advisable to do so.

....

Discuss your answers in small groups.

3 In the box below, write down another phrase from Exercise 2 which expresses each of the ideas:

Obligation	You have to do it.	....
No obligation	You're not obliged to do it.	....
Permission	You can do it.	....
Prohibition	You can't/cannot do it.	....
Moral obligation	★You're supposed to do it.	....

★ *Be supposed to is used to talk about a rule, custom or duty, and often has the force of a moral obligation.*

Example: *If you go to a funeral in Britain, you're supposed to wear dark colours.*

4 Using these phrases, write some more sentences about birth, marriage or death in your country.

Example: I*n my country, you have to get married in a church **and** a registry office.*

Show your sentences to a partner.

5 Are there any laws or customs in your country about birth, marriage or death that you disagree with? Discuss in groups.

1 Work in groups of four. Read one text each about a wedding ceremony (there are two on the next page), and then together answer the questions below. Use a dictionary if necessary.

Muslim Wedding
(in Saudi Arabia)

On the eve of the wedding, the bride's hands and feet are painted by her female relatives using henna dye. The ceremony can be conducted by any knowledgeable Muslim male, but an Imam usually leads it. Muslim men can marry Muslims or Christians; the women can marry only Muslims.

The wedding begins at 9.00 in the evening and goes on until about 4.00 in the morning. The bride usually wears a white dress and the groom a long white robe. During the ceremony the men and women are in separate rooms and sit or dance or listen to singing. After the ceremony, the guests are given a meal and at some weddings, they receive a gift.

Hindu Wedding

The wedding usually takes place in a hall where a canopy filled with flowers is set up by the bride's family. The bride arrives first in a red, green or white silk sari, with her friends and family. Then she is hidden away while everyone goes out to welcome the groom and his friends and relatives. Lights are waved over his head as he is taken under the canopy and the bride is brought to join him. The ceremony is followed by a meal for all the guests.

Orthodox Jewish Wedding

Before the ceremony the groom inspects the veiled bride in a separate room to make sure she is the woman he plans to marry. The wedding is then held under a canopy supported by four poles. Only the groom speaks during the ceremony, and wine is passed among family members. The groom then stamps on a glass and everyone wishes the couple good luck. Some couples go on honeymoon, but at a traditional wedding, the bride and groom are entertained at a party given by a different friend or relative every night for seven nights.

Japanese Wedding

Japanese couples don't have a list of wedding presents; friends and relatives are expected to give cash instead. During a typical Shinto ceremony, the bride wears a kimono and only the relatives of the bride and groom usually attend the actual ceremony. The groom drinks three sips of *sake* from a special bowl; it is then refilled and the bride drinks from the same bowl. Although many Japanese people have Shinto weddings, they usually have Buddhist funerals.

Are these sentences true or false? If false, correct the sentence.

1. All the wedding guests attend a Japanese wedding ceremony.
2. During a Jewish wedding ceremony the bride mustn't speak.
3. In Japan, friends and relatives are supposed to give the bride and groom money.
4. Muslim women are allowed to marry men from other religions.
5. At a Hindu wedding the couple have to perform a dance.

2 Now tell each member of the group more about the text you read. Are there any customs that appear in two different types of wedding?

3 Notice the use of the present simple passive in the texts:

Examples: *The wedding **is held** under a canopy.*
*The bride's hands and feet **are painted**.*

Rewrite these texts, using the passive twice in each text where it is appropriate. Compare your answers with a partner.

1. At a Sikh wedding reception, friends and relatives compose poems and speeches in honour of the couple; and people place banknotes in the couple's hands to ensure future prosperity.
2. In China, the couple consult astrological charts to fix the best time for the wedding. If the couple miss that date, they may have to wait years for another. Brides traditionally wear red, but white is becoming more common.
3. In parts of Africa, people expect the bride to cry before the ceremony; and they think that the more the bride cries, the happier she will be in her future life.

4 From all the wedding customs you have read about, which is the most attractive? Discuss in groups.

5 In groups, talk about weddings in your own culture. Is there anything special that the bride, the groom, or the parents:

- has/have to (do/wear/say, etc.)?
- is/are supposed to (do/wear/give, etc.)?
- doesn't/don't have to (say/make/do, etc.)?
- isn't/aren't allowed to (go/leave/do, etc.)?

PERSONAL STUDY WORKBOOK

In your Personal Study Workbook, you will find more exercises to help you with your learning. For Unit 9, these include:

- an exercise on passives
- vocabulary exercises on birth, marriage and death; and countries and nationalities
- a reading text about the minimum age you are allowed to do certain things in England and Wales
- a listening passage about wedding preparations
- another page of your visual dictionary to complete – about weddings and funerals

---

REVIEW AND DEVELOPMENT

REVIEW OF UNIT 7

1 Courses, butlers and actors | vocabulary |

Work in small groups.
Take turns to find pairs of words that are connected in some way. (You can use the same word in different connections.)

Example: *You can **sit** an **exam**.*

to sit	a subject	to pour	brilliant
a course	an exam	to handle	staff
to supervise	guests	a script	architecture
to fail	to apply for	a butler	to pass
hopeless	to deal with	a tray	to enrol
drinks	to register	a character	a certificate
agile	to carry	order	fitness

2 The most and the least ... | relative clauses |

Look at the underlined structures in the examples, then complete the sentences below *in your own words*. Compare your answers in groups. Are any of your sentences the same?

The person who/that	helps me most	
	I most admire	is my sister.
The person (who/that)	I see most often in my family	
The thing that	gives me most pleasure	
	I understand least in the world	is my computer.
The thing (that)	I use most often	

1. .... is my English book.
2. .... is my brother/sister.
3. .... is foreign travel.
4. .... is the leader of my country.
5. .... is sunbathing.
6. .... is money.

REVIEW OF UNIT 8

1 Let's not argue, but ... | link words: concession and addition |

A Work with a partner. Choose one of the topics in the illustrations.

living in a bedsit

owning a dog

being a man or woman

being in prison

having very long hair

a topic of your choice

Now work alone for a few minutes. One of you should write down four or five advantages; the other should write four or five disadvantages.

Example: *living alone*
        Advantages: *You can eat what you want, and when you want.*
                       You can leave the washing up for days, if you want.
                       You can make as much noise as you like (as long as the neighbours don't hear).
                       The bathroom is always free.
      Disadvantages: *It can be lonely.*
                       You may feel frightened alone at night.
                       You have to pay all the bills.
                       You often have no one to share your problems with when you get home.

B Now discuss your topic, using these phrases:

One of the main advantages of (living alone) is that ....

Another advantage is that ....

Yes, but on the other hand, ...

Another disadvantage is that ....

C When you have finished, find a new partner who chose a different topic. Tell them your topic and advantages and see if they can give you disadvantages on the spot.

2 Mostly to do with work ... | verb + noun collocations |

Work with a partner. Divide the phrases into two groups:

1. mostly to do with work (Example: *putting in a job application*)
2. to do with home or work (Example: *consulting people*)

giving someone orders   managing finances   reaching agreements
receiving sickness pay   making appointments   consulting colleagues
sharing problems with someone   making cutbacks   solving problems
having job security   getting paid holidays

Compare your answers with another pair.

10

PHONAHOLICS

Language focus:
used to do for past habits
what to say on the telephone

Vocabulary:
telephoning
phrasal verbs
hobbies and interests
synonyms

1 How many phone calls have you made in the last three days? Who were they to? What were they for? How long did they last? Discuss in groups, and find the most common reason for phoning.

2 Read the questionnaire and check the meaning of any new vocabulary. Then complete it on your own.

QUESTIONNAIRE:
USING THE PHONE

1 Which of these do you own, and why?

☐ an answering machine/ answerphone
☐ a fax machine
☐ a mobile phone
☐ a videophone

2 How often do you use these? Often, sometimes, hardly ever, never?

☐ A telephone directory
☐ Directory Enquiries
☐ International direct dialling
☐ Phone information services e.g. time, weather forecast
☐ Alarm/wake up calls
☐ Reversed charge calls ('Collect calls' in USA)

3 How often do these things happen?

☐ you dial the wrong number
☐ you get cut off in the middle of a call
☐ someone hangs up on you
☐ the number you ring is engaged
☐ you get a crossed line

4 Do you know and can you remember the phone numbers of the following ?

☐ all the members of your family
☐ your doctor
☐ your best friend
☐ your place of work

Which others do you know?

5 Are these sentences true for you?

☐ I really enjoy making and receiving phone calls.
☐ I sometimes let the phone ring without answering.
☐ I don't like leaving messages on answerphones.
☐ My life would be impossible without a phone.

6 In normal circumstances, what is the earliest or latest time you would ring a friend or member of the family?

☐ 7.00 am? 8.00 am? 9.00 am?
☐ 9.00 pm? 10.00 pm? 11.00 pm? or earlier or later than these?

Discuss your answers in groups.

3 We often confirm what someone says using different language. Can you confirm the information in the dialogues below using these phrasal verbs?

- *0* ring (someone) back
- *2* put off something
- *3* be/get cut off *go to off?*
- *1* hang up (on somebody)
- *5* get through (to somebody)
- *7* hang on
- *6* put someone through
- *4* wake (someone) up

Example: A: *She says she'll ring again this evening.*
B: *Oh, so she'll ring you back.*

1. 'He just put the phone down in the middle of the call.'
2. 'I should ring every Tuesday, but sometimes I don't phone until the Thursday or Friday.'
3. 'I was in the middle of the call and suddenly the phone went dead.'
4. 'He sounded terrible on the phone. I think he'd just got out of bed.'
5. 'I tried to phone them three or four times but it was hopeless.'
6. 'I often have problems and then the operator has to connect me.'
7. 'It's always the same. You ring them up and they tell you to wait.'

4 With a partner, choose two of your dialogues and continue them until a logical conclusion. Practise them, and then act them out for others in the group.

5 Work in small groups. Do any of the dialogues remind you of telephone situations that you often experience? If so, tell others about it.

MAKE THAT CALL!

1 In a phone conversation, who would say the phrases in the box:
   – the caller?
   – the person receiving the call?
   – an operator/receptionist?
   – any of them?

Speaking.   Is that Joanne?   It's Nigel.
Who's calling?   Could you give him a message?
Hold the line, please.   Is that you, Jo?
Shall I get him to ring you?
Do you know when they'll be back?
I'll put you through.   Hang on a minute.
Who shall I say is calling?   Thanks for ringing.
Could I speak to Mr Roberts, please?

2 **A** 💿 Listen to three conversations and complete the box.

	Relationship e.g. Boss/assistant	Language: Formal/informal	Reason for call
1.	....	....	....
2.	....	....	....
3.	....	....	....

B Listen again. Which phrases from Exercise 1 do you hear? Tick them and then compare with a partner.

3 Work with a partner. Write down three ways in which each of the conversations in Exercise 2 could continue.

Example: *Conversation 1:* **The caller accepts the appointment.**

4 💿 Now listen to the endings of the conversations. Were any of your guesses the same?

5 Work with a partner. Practise making calls. Your teacher will give you some role cards. Before you begin, think about these telephone tips carefully.

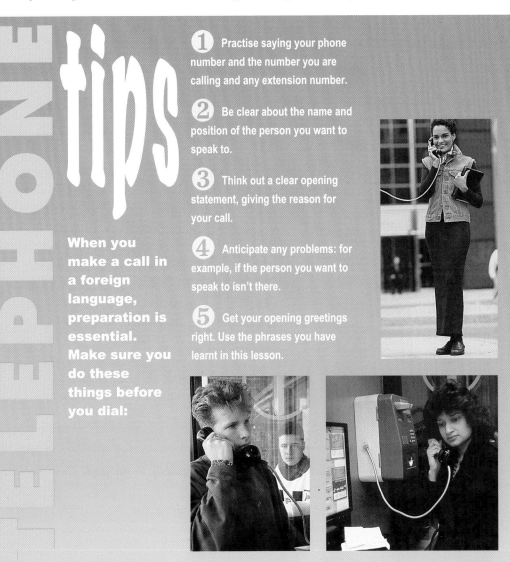

TELEPHONE tips

When you make a call in a foreign language, preparation is essential. Make sure you do these things before you dial:

1 Practise saying your phone number and the number you are calling and any extension number.

2 Be clear about the name and position of the person you want to speak to.

3 Think out a clear opening statement, giving the reason for your call.

4 Anticipate any problems: for example, if the person you want to speak to isn't there.

5 Get your opening greetings right. Use the phrases you have learnt in this lesson.

1 Find synonyms on the right for each of the words on the left.

deteriorate   sack
hostile   get worse
chat   unfriendly/aggressive
dismiss   safe/not damaging
install   conversation
harmless   fit

2 Read the story. Is there anything in it which is difficult to believe? Discuss with a partner and give reasons for your answer.

'My name is Jim Shelley and I am an addict ...'

With these words I began to solve the problem, the problem of my telephone addiction. You see, I used to phone, make calls, ring people up – talk, talk, talk. I used to call people all the time. From the moment I woke up to the time I went to sleep, I waited to be phoned, I wanted to phone. Just one more call.

It started socially I suppose – a few calls each day. It seemed harmless, just a quick chat. Gradually though, the situation got worse. Soon it was frequent use, then compulsive calling, until, finally, addiction.

And it began to affect my work. I was spending all of my lunchtime phoning. During the day I would disappear for a quick call. I spent days waiting for the phone to ring. I got agitated. In the end, I would ring someone, then someone else, telling myself 'just one more'.

I was phoning people and leaving messages to guarantee enough calls to see me through the day. I used to arrive at friends' homes and before the door was closed, go straight for the phone with the words 'Is it OK if I just use the phone ...?' One night I found it impossible to sleep, thinking I could hear the phone ringing downstairs. I jumped out of bed and then discovered it hadn't rung at all.

Things were so bad I often rang people and asked them if they had been trying to ring me. I had a business line and a private line installed. I bought an answerphone, then borrowed money so I could buy a car and have a carphone. At work, I became hostile and violent when colleagues tried to stop me using the phone. And one day I hit my supervisor (with the phone). I was dismissed and offered redundancy or one week's free calls which I accepted. Finally the police caught me destroying a phone box that had taken my last £1 coin, and I was ordered to see a psychiatrist.

I haven't had a phone in the house for three weeks now, and it's several days since I used a phone box. I also try not to watch TV because there are always people on it making phone calls. My name is James Shelley and I am an addict. I am an addict.

Please don't call me and I won't call you

3 *Used to + verb* is a form which describes something that happened *regularly in the past* or *was true for some time in the past* but is different, or not true now.

Examples: *In the days before the car was invented, people **used to travel** by horse or on foot.*
            (Now things are different.)
            *My father **used to have** a beard.*
            (He had one for some time, but he doesn't have one now.)

Notice that in the first example (for regular events), you can also use *would*:

*In the days before the car was invented, people **would travel** by horse or on foot.*

See Grammar Reference page 164 for more information.
Now look at the phrases underlined in the text. Where could you say *used to* instead, without changing the meaning?

Example: *The situation got worse.*
(You can't say *used to* in this example.)
I was spending all of my lunchtime phoning.
(= I *used to* spend …)

Compare with a partner. Transform the sentences you can change, using *used to*.

4 Work with a partner and imagine that you both *used to be* addicted to one of these activities. Write some confessions about things you used to do.

Example: *TV addiction*
I used to get up in the middle of the night and watch the TV.
I used to ring the office to say I was ill, and stay at home and watch the TV.
I used to eat all my meals in front of the TV.

writing your name on everything
buying make-up
physical exercise   chess
computers   crosswords
jigsaw puzzles

Make your confessions to the class.

PERSONAL STUDY WORKBOOK

In your Personal Study Workbook, you will find more exercises to help you with your learning. For Unit 10, these include:

- vocabulary exercises on compounds and wordbuilding
- practice of *used to do*
- phone conversations to listen to which practise vocabulary and useful phrases
- writing phone messages
- a speaking partners activity involving making phone calls

REVIEW OF UNIT 8

1 My words, your definition | vocabulary and paraphrasing |

Work with a partner and complete these definitions.

Example: *Being* self-employed *means* .you get money from your own business and you don't.
.have a boss.

People *receive sickness pay* when ....

If you work *flexible* hours, it means ....

Having *a day off* means ....

If you *give someone orders* it means ....

If you *lack* something, you ....

If you have *job security*, then you ....

Compare your definitions with another pair. Which are the best definitions? Now look at a monolingual dictionary. Is your definition better, or not?

2 Managers discuss training budgets | pronunciation: word stress |

Work with a partner. Put the words into the correct circle based on the main stress.

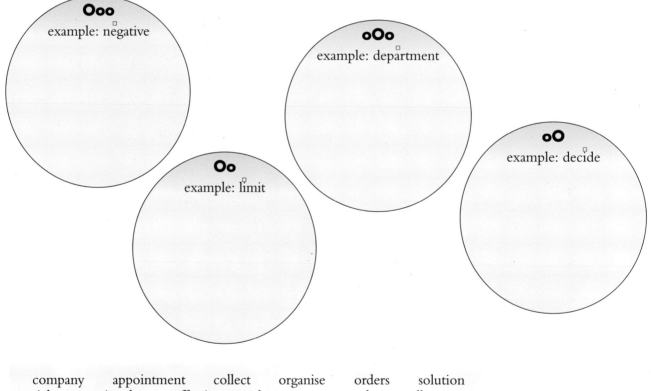

Ooo
example: negative

oOo
example: department

Oo
example: limit

oO
example: decide

company	appointment	collect	organise	orders	solution
sickness	involve	effective	advantage	consult	colleague
difficult	positive	agreement	training	employed	discuss
cutbacks	financial	manager	flexible	budget	accept

⊡ Listen to the recording to check your answers.
With a partner, make up three sentences using at least two of the words above in each one.

Example: *The financial manager wanted to discuss cutbacks.*

Listen to another pair's sentences. Are they pronouncing the words correctly?

REVIEW OF UNIT 9

1 Bridal quiz | vocabulary and speaking |

Answer the following questions. Work in groups.

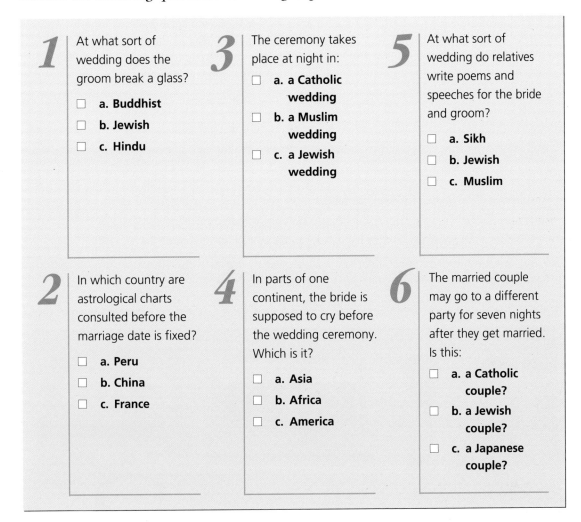

1 At what sort of wedding does the groom break a glass?
- ☐ **a. Buddhist**
- ☐ **b. Jewish**
- ☐ **c. Hindu**

3 The ceremony takes place at night in:
- ☐ **a. a Catholic wedding**
- ☐ **b. a Muslim wedding**
- ☐ **c. a Jewish wedding**

5 At what sort of wedding do relatives write poems and speeches for the bride and groom?
- ☐ **a. Sikh**
- ☐ **b. Jewish**
- ☐ **c. Muslim**

2 In which country are astrological charts consulted before the marriage date is fixed?
- ☐ **a. Peru**
- ☐ **b. China**
- ☐ **c. France**

4 In parts of one continent, the bride is supposed to cry before the wedding ceremony. Which is it?
- ☐ **a. Asia**
- ☐ **b. Africa**
- ☐ **c. America**

6 The married couple may go to a different party for seven nights after they get married. Is this:
- ☐ **a. a Catholic couple?**
- ☐ **b. a Jewish couple?**
- ☐ **c. a Japanese couple?**

You will find all the answers in Unit 9, so go back and check if you can't remember.

2 In my country ... | obligation, permission and prohibition |

A Think about these questions.

1. In your country, do you have to ...
   - do military service?
   - vote in national elections?
   - have lessons from a driving school when you learn to drive?
   - show your diplomas/certificates when you apply for a job?
   - carry some form of identification on you?
   - have a licence for a bicycle?

2. In your country, are you allowed to ...
   - smoke on public transport?
   - drive a car without insurance?
   - buy cigarettes under the age of 16?
   - ride a motorbike without a crash helmet?
   - own a dog without a licence?

Now ask and answer the questions in small groups, and discuss any differences.

GOODS AND SERVICES

Language focus:	Vocabulary:
if sentences with *will, may* or *might* *have something done*	electrical appliances and other consumer goods clothes and shopping suffixes: *-able, -ible*

A HARD SELL   *if sentences with will, may, might; vocabulary: consumer goods*

1 When you buy something in a shop, the sales assistant may try to sell you a related item.

Example: *If you buy a tape recorder, the sales assistant will probably ask you if you need any blank tapes.*
If you buy a tennis racket, they may/might try to sell you tennis balls at the same time.

List the things a sales assistant *will* or *may/might* try to sell you if you buy the items below. Work in small groups and use dictionaries if necessary.

Example: *a cassette recorder* <u>headphones, microphone, blank tapes</u>

a torch ....
a man's shirt ....
a woman's handbag ....
a camera ....
a table lamp ....
a bicycle ....
a home computer ....
an expensive ballpoint pen ....
a pair of shoes ....
a washing machine ....

Tell the class your answers using full sentences, as in the examples.

2 A good sales assistant must also know about the features and benefits of their products. With a partner, add as much as you can to the table below.

Product	Features	Benefits
Levi jeans	strong cotton	They will last a long time.
	dark grey	....
	loose fit	....
	pre-shrunk	....
Car radio/cassette	portable	....
	10 station memory	....
	4 speakers	....
	12 month guarantee	....

3 In groups, write a similar table of features and benefits for one or two of these products, or choose your own.

a pair of trainers   an alarm clock   an electronic dictionary   a travelling bag

4 Show your descriptions to other groups. Can they add any other features and benefits?

CUSTOMER SERVICE
have something done; vocabulary: shopping

1 Is there anything in this text which would be unacceptable or unusual in your country?

You took a friend shopping in the nearest large town.

First you went to a street market where your friend wanted to buy a melon. She offered the seller 30% less than he wanted. She then bought two kilos of oranges.

After that, you went around the local shops, and your friend saw some fabric she liked. Again, she offered less than the asking price. She asked if she could have a dress made from the fabric by the following day.

Next, you went into a department store, and your friend tried on some earrings, but didn't buy them. In the women's fashion department, she tried on a skirt which she liked but it was rather long. She asked if she could have it shortened free of charge. In the end, she tried to pay for the skirt in traveller's cheques.

Your friend then took you down to the china department because she wanted to buy you a present. She told you to choose anything you wanted. You chose a set of wine glasses and this time she wanted to pay with a credit card and have them delivered to your home.

Finally, you went to a sweet shop and your friend bought a large box of locally-made sweets to take home for a friend. She wanted to have them gift-wrapped.

Discuss your answers in groups.

A HARD SELL

2 In the text the friend wanted *to have things done*. For example, she wanted to:

have	*object*	*past participle*
have	a dress	made
have	a skirt	shortened
have	some glasses	delivered
have	a present	gift-wrapped

You can use this construction when someone provides a service for you, which you sometimes pay for. Can you have the following services provided in your country? Tell a partner.

Example: *In my country you can't have a suit made in 24 hours – it usually takes a long time – but you can have milk delivered to your home.*

Can you …
- have milk and newspapers delivered to your home?
- have a suit or dress made in 24 hours?
- have your shoes cleaned in public?
- have your shopping delivered to your home?
- have items gift-wrapped in a shop free of charge?
- have a phone installed within a week?
- have your car windows cleaned at a petrol station?
- have your eyes tested free of charge?
- have a film developed in less than an hour?
- have your portrait painted in the street?
- have your dog walked?

3 In groups, make a list of at least three things that you can *have done* in these places. Use a dictionary if necessary.

1. a hairdresser's   2. a garage   3. a doctor's surgery

CAN YOU SELL IT?   suffixes: *-able*, *-ible*

1 Look at the two pictures. What does *portable* mean?

> It's portable.

> … and of course you can carry this TV around with you to any room in the house

With a partner, write the *long* explanation for each of these words.

disposable   inflatable   washable   reversible   unbreakable   edible
adjustable   lockable   detachable

Where is the stress on these words? Can you work out a rule?

2 Which of the words could you use to describe these things?

3 Read the advertisements below and decide which item is the most unusual, and which you would like to have. Tell a partner.

DISPOSABLE SUITS!

At LAST, an end to dry cleaning bills. Soil our suits and you simply THROW THEM AWAY!!!! Lightweight suits *Also available in tweed.* state size and style when ordering.

FAIRLY LONG LASTING CONTAINS NO CFC'S

£25 PER DOZ

REVERSIBLE TROUSERS

For Men and boys

Change your trousers instantly anywhere! anytime! and surprise your friends.

AVAILABLE IN ALL SIZES

TWO for £14.99
Satisfaction guaranteed or your money back.

TRAVELLING SET OF ENCYCLOPEDIAS

£25.99

This easy to carry portable set of encyclopedias means you never have to get caught short on holiday again.

A BOON TO THE MODERN TRAVELLER. PRINT NAME AND ADDRESS CLEARLY ON ORDER.

☐ 4947....

REINFORCED ODOURLESS SOXS

The original guaranteed odourless sox. Take your shoes off in public and see the relief on your friends' faces. £2.50 a pair.

4 With your partner answer these questions.

1. What is the advantage of the socks? What can you do if you are wearing them?
2. What are the financial advantages of the suits? Are they all the same?
3. What is the advantage of the encyclopedias?
4. What is special about the trousers? Are they suitable for anyone?

5 ⬚⬚ ⬚⬚ On the recording you will hear someone trying to sell one of the products. Which one? Are they successful, and what advantages does the person mention?

6 Work with a partner. One of you should look at page 171, the other at page 173. Read your advert, then try to sell the product to your partner.

PERSONAL STUDY WORKBOOK

In your Personal Study Workbook, you will find more exercises to help you with your learning. For Unit 11, these include:

- vocabulary exercises on suffixes and product features
- reading about legal rights
- an exercise on *if* sentences
- writing a letter of complaint
- another page of your visual dictionary – clothes and electrical appliances

---

REVIEW AND DEVELOPMENT

REVIEW OF UNIT 9

1 Our island | obligation and prohibition |

Welcome to our island in

....
(name of sea/ocean)

called ....

PLEASE OBEY OUR LAWS

Work in groups of three or four. You are the rulers of a small island. Write down some of the laws and customs you would like to have.

On our island you have to:
1. ....
2. ....
3. ....

And on our island you aren't allowed to:
1. ....
2. ....
3. ....

And you don't have to:
1. ....
2. ....
3. ....

Read your laws and customs to another group and discuss them.

2 Similar but different   vocabulary: stages in life

Look at the pairs of sentences below. How are the underlined words different in meaning or style? Use a dictionary and work with your partner.

Example: a. *We live next door to an <u>old</u> man.*
         b. *We live next door to an <u>elderly</u> man.*
'Elderly' is more polite than 'old' in this case.

1. a. They've got three <u>children</u>.
   b. They've got <u>triplets</u>.
2. a. Do you like <u>kids</u>?
   b. Do you like <u>children</u>?
3. a. We saw a <u>young person</u> running out of the shop.
   b. We saw a <u>youth</u> running out of the shop.
4. a. This party is only for <u>adults</u>.
   b. This party is only for <u>grown-ups</u>.
5. a. That child is <u>growing up</u> fast.
   b. That child is <u>growing</u> fast.
6. a. She's got a class of <u>adolescents</u>.
   b. She's got a class of <u>teenagers</u>.

⫇ Listen to the recording and check your answers.

REVIEW OF UNIT 10

1 He used to stand on his head   used to + verb

Think of people who were in charge of you in the past, e.g. a school teacher and a previous boss. What were their bad habits or mannerisms? Tell each other in groups.

Examples: *My boss used to repeat herself all the time.*
                      look out of the window when he talked to me.
          I had a teacher who used to tell us stupid jokes.
                      sit on the floor.

2 On the phone   speaking

Read the information below, while a partner reads the information on page 172. Then practise the three phone conversations together.

1. You are Mr Cartwright's secretary. He is quite busy this morning and he will only speak to the Personnel Manager. Other callers will have to leave a message or ring him back.
2. You phone your friend. You want to meet them for a meal at the weekend because you haven't seen them for several months.
3. You ring your friend Josephine. You need to contact her to get the address of her lawyer.

BARE NECESSITIES

Language focus:
describing degrees of need
frequency and degree adverbs
qualifying adjectives
numbers and measurements

Vocabulary:
climate and geography
toiletries
personal belongings

I COULD MANAGE WITHOUT IT   describing degrees of need; household vocabulary

1 Here are some things that British people sometimes own but only need on certain occasions. Why might they need them?

> a barbecue   Christmas decorations   candles   a sleeping bag   cuff links
> a torch   a beach umbrella   mosquito spray   an electric fan   a trunk

Do you think people in your country would own these things? If so, would they use them regularly, occasionally or would they rarely use them? Discuss in groups.

2 In your home, where do you keep the things you don't use very often? Tell a partner.

> in a store cupboard   in a cellar   in the basement   in the attic   in a spare room
> in a shed   under a bed   somewhere else

3 Listen to two people talking about things they don't use very often. Complete the table.

	Things they want to keep	Things they can manage without	Things they would like to get rid of
Speaker 1	....	....	....
Speaker 2	....	....	....

Compare your answers with a partner.

4 In groups, tell each other about the things you keep in store. Are they things you need? Could you manage without them? Would you like to get rid of them?

5 Think of something you own but would like to swap for something else. Then take a sheet of paper, and write down what you've got, and what kind of thing you would like to swap it/them for.

Example:

> I've got a large collection of classical music cassettes which I don't use because I now have a CD player. I would like to swap some of them for some clothes or CDs or jewellery.

Display your notices around the room. Read them all and see if you can find a swap.

ICE BREAKS
climate and geography; numbers and measurements

1 Complete this mind map with words from the box, and make sure you understand all the items.

| typhoon | melt | drizzle | stream | boil | pond | flood | lightning | sleet |

2 Imagine you were going to stay in a hotel which is a giant igloo (a house made of icy blocks of snow). Would these be advantages or disadvantages?

It might melt.
It would be very light.
It would be a novelty.
It would be pretty chilly.

With a partner, think of one more advantage and disadvantage, then tell the rest of the class.

3 Read the text. Why does Nils Bergqvist think the igloo hotel is a good idea? Compare your answers with a partner.

ICE BREAKS

Holiday makers who are bored with baking beaches and overheated hotel rooms head for a giant igloo.

Swedish businessman Nils Bergqvist is delighted with the response to his new accommodation concept, the world's first igloo hotel. Built in Jukkasjärvi, a small town in Lapland, it has been attracting lots of visitors, but soon the fun will be over.

In two weeks' time Bergqvist's ice creation will be nothing more than a pool of water. 'We don't see melting as a big problem,' he says. 'We just look forward to making a bigger and more beautiful one to replace it.'

Bergqvist built his first igloo in 1991 for a local art exhibition. It was so successful that he designed the current one, which measures roughly 200 square metres. Six workmen spent more than eight weeks piling 1,000 tons of snow onto a wooden base; when the snow froze, the base was removed. 'The only wooden thing we have left in the igloo is the front door,' he says. Everything else is 100 per cent snow, including a chapel with seats covered in reindeer fur.

Bed and breakfast in one of the ice cubicles is £25–£30 per night. After their stay, all visitors receive a survival certificate recording their accomplishment. With no doors, nowhere to hang clothes and temperatures around 0°C, it may seem more like an endurance test than a relaxing hotel break. 'It's a great novelty for them,' Bergqvist explains, 'as well as being a good start in survival training.' He says that guests feel warm despite the cold because snow is such a good insulator. Maximum heat is maintained by ice walls that are about two metres thick.

The popularity of the resort is beyond doubt: it is now attracting tourists from all over the world. At least 800 people have stayed at the igloo this season even though there are only 10 rooms. 'You can get a lot of people in,' explains Bergqvist. 'The beds are three metres wide by two metres long, and can fit at least four at one time.'

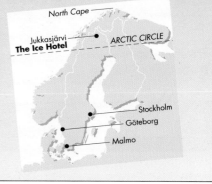

Would you like to stay in this hotel? Tell your partner, and say why or why not.

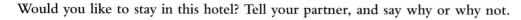

4 In the text, there are various numbers and measurements. Go back and underline them, and then compare with a partner.

5 Try this short quiz with a partner. Then write two more similar questions and give them to another pair to answer.

1. An Olympic swimming pool is .... metres long by .... metres wide, and the water is at least .... deep at the shallow end.
2. The digestive tract in the human body is about .... metres long and it can take food a maximum of .... hours to pass through it.
3. Water boils at .... degrees centigrade at sea level.
4. A tennis court measures approximately .... square metres.
5. Human skin is about .... thick.
6. Roughly ....% of the earth's surface is covered by water.
7. The external walls of a modern house are roughly .... centimetres thick.
8. A bird's heart beats at approximately .... times a minute.

1 You are on a long night flight and the airline gives you the items below. Which phrase in the box describes your reaction to each one?

> absolutely essential   very useful   quite useful   not very useful   completely unnecessary

> a flannel   ear plugs   a nail-file   socks   cologne   a shoehorn
> toothpaste   tissues   an eyemask   a comb   a clothes brush
> a 'don't disturb' sticker

Compare your answers in groups.

2 Do you know when to use *absolutely* and *very* before adjectives? Here are some more examples. ✓ means *correct* and ✗ means *incorrect*. Can you find a rule and then correct the mistakes? Work with a partner.

absolutely fantastic ✓   very good ✓
absolutely freezing ✓   very cold ✓
absolutely big ✗   very enormous ✗
absolutely nice ✗   very delicious ✗

3 Which word would you use before these adjectives? Work with a partner and use a dictionary if necessary.

....	hot	....	exhausted
....	bad	....	dreadful
....	boiling	....	tired
....	furious	....	unbelievable
....	angry	....	useless

4 Prepare a dialogue with a partner around this situation, using language from Exercises 2 and 3.

Your plane has just landed after a dreadful ten-hour flight, and your partner is at the airport to meet you. Tell them all the things that went wrong.

Practise your dialogue with your partner, and then act it for another pair.

5 ▭ Airlines may also offer you some more unusual items on your flight. Listen and write down at least three more. Compare your answers with a partner and discuss which ones you would like to receive.

PERSONAL STUDY WORKBOOK

In your Personal Study Workbook, you will find more exercises to help you with your learning. For Unit 12, these include:

- practice of adjectives and adverbs
- compound words and collocations
- a text about the strange things people carry in their handbags
- an exercise to help you make your writing more interesting
- another page of your visual dictionary to complete – in an attic

---

REVIEW AND DEVELOPMENT

REVIEW OF UNIT 10

1 On the phone   listening

▭ Listen to these six phone calls. Write down in a sentence what happens in each one.

1. ....
2. ....
3. ....
4. ....
5. ....
6. ....

2 Sounds and spelling | pronunciation |

Underline all the examples of /ɪ/ (as in *sit*) and circle all the examples of /aɪ/ (as in *side*) in these words.

| hostile | business | dial | tried | addict | mobile | dialogue | aggressive |
| message | promise | exercise | anticipate | minute (time) | supervisor |

📼 Listen and check your answers. Then practise saying them with a partner.

REVIEW OF UNIT 11

1 Everyday items | vocabulary |

On page 74, you thought of goods which a sales assistant would try to sell you in addition to the main item you were buying. For instance, if you bought a tennis racket, they might try to sell you tennis balls.
From the related goods below, what do you think the main item could be? Discuss with a partner.

Example: *blank cassettes* **cassette recorder or video recorder**

1. ribbons and paper
2. a refill
3. a puncture kit
4. polish and tights
5. batteries
6. a tie
7. gloves and a purse
8. blank disks, paper and software
9. a light bulb
10. flash, lenses and filters

2 Have you had your hair cut? | have something done |

Make sentences using words from each column, with the construction *have something done*, and in the correct tense. Try to use all the words and expressions.

Example: *I haven't had my eyes tested this year.*
     or
     I have my eyes tested every five years.

If you *do it yourself*, use a different construction:

Example: *I painted my house two years ago.*

Noun	Verb	Time expression
eyes	develop	next week
house	service	every six months
curtains	cut	this year
film	test	once a year
watch	install	two years ago
hair	repair	every five years
central heating	clean	yesterday
car	paint	for six weeks

Discuss your answers in small groups.

WHO IS REALLY ON TRIAL?

Language focus:
if sentences with *would* and *might*
defining relative clauses (2)
link words: similarities and differences

Vocabulary:
law and the legal system
crime

CRIME PREVENTION   vocabulary: *if* sentences with *would* and *might*

CLOSED CIRCUIT TELEVISION
SURVEILLANCE IN OPERATION

1 Organise the vocabulary items below into three groups
in your notebook:

Words I know   Words I'm not sure about   Words I don't know

> to steal   to burgle   burglar   burglary   burglar alarm   theft   thief
> to commit a crime   criminal   street lighting   unemployment   to reduce
> a tough punishment   leisure centre   drug trafficking   to protect
> young offenders   property   warehouse   jail   victim

Work in small groups and compare your lists. Help each other with columns two and
three, and use a dictionary. When you understand a word, add it to column 1, and
continue until all the words are in column 1.

2 Read the short text, then either tick (✓) sentences in the speech bubbles that you agree with or. put a cross (✗) if you disagree.

CRIME

In many countries, most crimes are 'crimes of property': stealing from shops, warehouses and homes as well as stealing cars and car radios. Often, these crimes are committed by young offenders, some of whom are under the age when they can be sent to jail. So what can be done? We gave members of the public some suggestions for reducing crime. Here are their reactions:

> If there were more police on the streets, there would be less crime.
>
> If people protected their property using dogs, it might make a difference.

> If there were tougher punishments for all crimes, it would make a very big difference.
>
> If all governments managed to stop drug trafficking, it might make a difference.

> If every home had a burglar alarm, it wouldn't make any difference at all.
>
> If young people had more leisure centres, it would reduce crime.

> If the streets had better lighting, it wouldn't make any difference.
>
> If the government reduced unemployment, there would be very little crime.

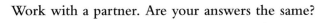

Work with a partner. Are your answers the same?

3 Look again at the sentences in the speech bubbles. For each one, circle the verb after *if* and underline the verb after the comma, as in the example.
Now answer these questions.

1. What tense follows *if*?
2. What verbs are used in the second part of the sentence?
3. What is being discussed: crime in the past, or crime now and in the future?
4. Do the sentences talk about situations that exist or situations that are imagined?

Compare your answers with your partner.

4 Look again at your ticks and crosses. Where you disagreed with a sentence, rewrite the second part so that you do agree with it.

Example: *If the streets had better lighting, it* ~~*wouldn't make any difference.*~~ *would make a big difference where I live.*

Now discuss your new sentences in small groups. Explain your reasons.

5 Complete these sentences in your own words, using the correct verb forms.

1. If the police had better computer information, ...
   ....

2. If more money were spent on education and training, ...
   ....

3. If prisoners had to meet their victims as part of their punishment, ...
   ....

4. It would make a big difference if ....

5. It might reduce the number of crimes if ....

6. It wouldn't make any difference if ....

Discuss your answers in small groups.

ADVICE FROM SOMEONE WHO KNOWS   link words: similarities and differences

1 What do you imagine life in prison is like? What do you think the daily routine is? Discuss in groups and then write down your ideas.

2 ▭ The man on the recording is a reformed criminal called John, who now spends much of his time telling young people about the dangers of crime. Listen and decide if these statements are true or false according to the speaker.

1. He spent twenty-five years in prison.
2. He was a burglar.
3. Life in prison is hard both physically and emotionally.
4. There is not much variety in the food.
5. Prisoners do nothing all day.
6. Prisoners can receive visitors once a week.

I think that's enough for today. See you tomorrow.

CRIME
DOES it PAY?

3 There are other situations where people's daily lives usually follow a strict routine:

- being a patient in hospital
- being in the army
- being at boarding school (you live at the school during term)

There are also differences. Read these examples and complete the remaining sentences in your own words.

1. In prison it is the same routine throughout the year **whereas** at boarding school things change in the holidays.
2. In prison you're locked in your room at night **whereas** in hospital ....
   ....
3. The army is **similar to** hospital, **except that** in the army, you move around more.
4. The army is **similar to** prison, **except that** in the army, ...
   ....
5. The army is **different from** prison **in that** you can do what you want in your free time.
6. Boarding school is **different from** the army, **in that** ....
   ....

Work with a partner. Can you think of any other differences between the institutions?

4 🎧 Listen to the second extract. In it, John describes what people can do to protect their homes from burglars. Make notes on his advice, then compare with a partner.

5 Work with the same partner. Make a poster about protecting your home or about protecting your car from theft using the ideas on the recording and your own ideas. When you are happy with it, put it up on the wall for others in your class to read.

Example: *Leave your lights on in winter.*

1 Look at the pictures. Can you identify ...

- the court?
- the person on trial (the defendant)?
- the judge?
- lawyers for the prosecution/defence?
- the jury/jurors?
- a witness?

2 In some countries there is a jury system for many criminal trials: people are judged by members of the public (usually twelve). Do you have the same system in your country? If not, how is it different? Discuss in groups.

3 Not everyone believes the jury system is a good idea. Work with a partner. One of you should read the text on this page, while the other reads the text on page 172.

The jury system on trial

In the past, jury service was an important duty, but one of the problems nowadays is that jurors don't take this duty seriously. Recent examples include a young woman juror who celebrated her birthday with so many lunchtime drinks that she couldn't continue with the trial in the afternoon. Another juror was found filling in a job application form during a trial; both jurors were given a fine by the judge.

Nowadays many of the people who do it think that it is inconvenient, often a waste of time, and a loss of income (jurors only receive a small sum of money for jury duty). Sometimes they have good reason to dislike it. Many jurors have to wait for days in unpleasant waiting rooms, and then sit for weeks in an uncomfortable courtroom on a hard chair.

Some members of the legal profession are also worried about the ability of some jurors. In longer trials, many professional people find ways to be excused, and so you often find that juries contain some people who cannot read very well, and juries do not always have enough 'well-educated' people who can understand what is happening.

There is also the cost: the payment of jurors is not a lot for the individual, but costs the country over £30m a year.

With your partner, make lists using the information in the texts of the advantages and disadvantages of the jury system. Add any further ideas of your own.

4 Match the sentence halves. Then compare with your partner.

1. A jury is a group of people who	a. defends or prosecutes.
2. A lawyer is a person who	b. decide if someone is guilty or innocent.
3. A fine is the money which	c. trials take place.
4. A court is the place where	d. sentences a criminal.
5. Witnesses are the people who	e. is paid as a punishment.
6. A judge is the person who	f. tell the court what they know about a crime.

Study the sentences for one minute. Then test each other, like this:

Example: A: *A judge is the person who* …
              B: *Sentences a criminal.*

5 Look at the sentences again. When do we use *who*, *which* or *where*?
Now complete these definitions, using *who*, *which* or *where*. Compare your definitions in small groups and with a dictionary.

A criminal is …	A jail is …	A leisure centre is …
A burglar alarm is …	A young offender is …	A burglar is …

PERSONAL STUDY WORKBOOK

In your Personal Study Workbook, you will find more exercises to help you with your learning. For Unit 13, these include:

- exercises on *if* sentences and relative clauses
- vocabulary to do with crime
- a writing exercise on combining sentences
- listening and reading activities on crime prevention
- questions about crime to discuss with your speaking partner

---

REVIEW AND DEVELOPMENT

REVIEW OF UNIT 11

1 Choose the right answer | *if sentences with will or would* |

Complete these sentences with: *if* + present simple, + *will*
                                                    or
                                                    if + past simple, + *would.*

In three of the sentences, you can use either construction. Which three?

1. If birds .... (not have) wings, they .... (not be) able to fly.
2. I .... (be) very unhappy if I .... (not have) so many friends.
3. If it .... (be) cold again tomorrow, we .... (have to) stay at home.
4. If we .... (not leave) now, we .... (miss) the beginning of the film.
5. I .... (be) very surprised if you .... (not like) the film.
6. I .... (see) him tomorrow if I .... (be) here, but in fact I'll be in Germany.
7. I .... (take) you out for dinner this evening if you .... (like).
8. If I .... (go) to Switzerland, ... (need) a raincoat?

Compare your answers with a partner.

2 Listen and answer vocabulary

📼 Listen and answer the questions. At the end you can check your answers with Tapescript 1 on page 174.

REVIEW OF UNIT 12

1 Let's measure it! numbers and measurements

A Have a guess at the answers to these questions.

1. The classroom is about .... metres long by .... metres wide, so it's around .... square metres.
2. The ceiling is about .... metres high.
3. The walls are probably about .... centimetres thick.
4. The board is roughly .... by ....

Compare your answers in groups. If possible, check them using a tape measure.

B Write down approximate measurements for some things in your room, but don't say what they are:

Example: *X is fifty centimetres by thirty centimetres.*
          Y is three centimetres thick.

Can others guess what the things are?

2 What would you do with that? verbs

Work with a partner. What can you see in the pictures?

What would you do if someone gave you the things in the pictures?
Tell your partner about each one, using the language in the table.
Explain your reasons.

I	would might	get rid of it/them. try to sell it/them. keep it/them. swap it/them with someone for something else. throw it/them away. put it/them away and forget about it/them. give it/them away. use it/them straightaway.

TALL STORIES, SHORT STORIES

Language focus:
past perfect simple
making excuses and reassuring
purpose, reason and result

Vocabulary:
the countryside
action verbs
transport
reasons for being late

THE FACE ON THE WALL   *past perfect*

1 What is the difference between a *short story* and a *tall story*? Use a dictionary to find out.

2 You are going to hear a man telling a story to a group of people. First, look at the picture and make sure you understand the first paragraph of the story.

It all started just over a year ago. I was staying in an old house in Great Ormond Street which had large patches of damp on the walls. And you know, one of these patches looked exactly like a human face. I used to sit and watch it and became so fascinated with it that I began to believe there must be a real person with a face like it. My search quickly became an obsession. I watched crowds of people all day long ... some must have thought I was mad, and even the police began to look at me suspiciously. Then one day ...

☐☐ Now listen to the first part of the story and find out what happened next.

THE FACE ON THE WALL   93

3 Look at this summary of the narrative. Each sentence contains an error of fact. Correct them and compare with a partner.

1. The storyteller followed the man to the coach station where he met two women and a girl.
2. He followed them to France, and when they arrived in Boulogne the storyteller asked the man for his card.
3. The man's name was Mr Ormond Wall and he came from Australia.
4. When he got back to England, the storyteller learnt that the man was a millionaire whose parents had lived in France.
5. When he went to sleep that evening, he noticed the face on the wall was difficult to see.
6. He went out and bought a paper which said that the millionaire had been in a train accident.
7. When he got home, he looked at the face on the wall, and suddenly it got darker again.
8. He learnt later that Mr Ormond Wall had left hospital at exactly the same moment.

4 〇〇 There are three extraordinary things about the story. What are they? Discuss with a partner, and then listen to the final part of the recording.
Is this a short story, a tall story or both?

5 Look at these sentences from the story:

1. He discovered that Mr Wall was a millionaire with English parents who <u>had lived</u> in London.
2. Later he found out that the man <u>had died</u> at exactly the same moment.

The verbs underlined are in the past perfect tense (*had* + past participle). It is often used to show the order in which events happened in a story.

Two verbs in this short text should also be in the past perfect. Which two? Discuss with a partner, using the time line to help you.

When Tom got back to the campsite with the milk and eggs he bought at the farm shop nearby, Mary was still in the tent. Fortunately they collected plenty of wood earlier, so Tom lit the fire immediately and started preparing the dinner.

We enter the story here

Unit 14 TALL STORIES, SHORT STORIES

6 Work with a partner. Give two possible explanations for each of these questions. One must be in the past perfect, the other in the past simple.

Example: *Why did she go to the police station?*
*Because she **had lost** her handbag.*
*Because she **wanted** some information about burglar alarms.*

2. Why did she leave her job?

1. Why did he take a taxi?

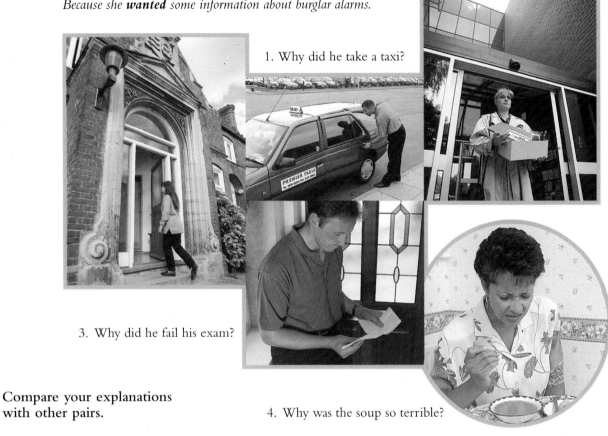

3. Why did he fail his exam?

Compare your explanations with other pairs.

4. Why was the soup so terrible?

CAN COMPUTERS TELL STORIES?

vocabulary: the countryside; purpose, reason, result

1 Work with a partner. In two or three sentences, write a story about the goat and the eagle in this picture, using a dictionary if necessary. When you have finished, show your story to another pair.

THE FACE ON THE WALL

2 Compare your story with the one in this text. Then read the rest of the text and answer the questions below.

Making fun of grammar

'Once upon a time an old mountain goat called Herbert lived in a cave. He was dirty and clever with short twisted horns, and every day hunger forced him out of the cave to look for food.

"Where shall I go today," thought Herbert. Suddenly an idea came to him and with hope in his heart he set off in search of food ...'

Unfortunately Herbert did not have much luck. An eagle swooped down and attacked him before he could eat his meal.

This story was written by a computer program, with the help of a nine-year-old mind to add a bit of imagination. The program creates plots for simple stories and teaches children how stories are structured using video-game techniques. This helps to transform grammar from something which many children hate into something which is fun.

For Herbert's story, the user is invited to type in a boy's name (Herbert), animal type (mountain goat), where he might live (cave), adjectives describing the animal (dirty, clever, with short twisted horns), and the program then produces a little story. Of course, nine-year-olds being what they are, the stories can end up being rather rude. One boy wanted Herbert to wear underpants, but he was later persuaded by the girls to change it to a pale blue T-shirt instead.

True or false? If the sentences are false, correct them.

1. The children write a story and the computer corrects their grammar.
2. The structure of the story is given by the computer.
3. The children type in some of the vocabulary.
4. They find the activity enjoyable.

What's your opinion? Is this good for children's learning, do you think? Discuss with a partner.

3 Work with a partner. Look up any new words on the computer screen, and then choose a word from each column to make sentences, as in the example. You must use all the words on the screen once only.

Example: *The children dived into the lake and swam to the other side.*

Subject	Action	Place	Purpose (to …) Reason (because …) or Result (and …/but …)
children	gallop	lake	
pilot	dive	path	
soldier	hop	cliff	
sparrow	land	woods	
motorbike	creep	lawn	
helicopter	kid	fence	
horse	crash	bushes	

4 Now choose two of the subjects, and see how many sentences you can generate, using different actions and places.

5 With your partner, write a simple story using two of your sentences. Include the names of two learners in your class. Read your story to another pair.

1 ▢▢ ▢▢ Most people have a story to tell about being late for something. Listen to the two stories on the recording and answer these questions.

    1. Where was each person going?
    2. Why were they late?
    3. What happened at the end?
    4. Do you think each story is true or *a tall story*?

Compare with a partner, then listen and find out if the stories were true or not.

2 Read these excuses for being late and check any new words in your dictionary. Which excuses did you hear in Exercise 1?

I'm sorry I'm late but …
  − the car/train/bus broke down.
  − there was a bus strike.
  − I got held up in the traffic.
  − I missed the bus.
  − my train was cancelled.
  − my alarm clock didn't go off.
  − I got off the bus at the wrong stop.
  − I bumped into an old friend on the way here.
  − I had a puncture/a flat tyre.
  − I got lost.
  − I overslept.
  − when I got to the station, I realised I'd left my money at home.

With a partner, add two more excuses that people use. Then compare with other pairs.

3 Which of the excuses have you used occasionally or regularly? Discuss in groups.

4 Look at this list of replies. Which can you use if someone makes an excuse for being late?

    Never mind.   I don't mind.   It doesn't matter.   That's all right.   I don't care.
    Don't worry.   Nothing.   It's not important.

5 Work with a partner. Write out a situation in which someone arrives late, and suggest one or two reasons.

Example: *You have a very important meeting with a new client at a hotel in the centre of town. You have a puncture, so you change the tyre, but you get so dirty that you have to go home and change your clothes. You arrive 40 minutes late.*

Change papers with another pair. Act out the situation they give you.

PERSONAL STUDY WORKBOOK

In your Personal Study Workbook, you will find more exercises to help you with your learning. For Unit 14, these include:

- an exercise on the past perfect and past simple
- practice in making excuses in different situations
- vocabulary exercises on collocation and wordbuilding
- another short story to read and listen to
- an exercise using link words to connect events

REVIEW AND DEVELOPMENT

REVIEW OF UNIT 12

1 Absolutely fabulous | pronunciation: intonation |

A Complete these sentences in a suitable way.

Examples: <u>My homework yesterday was</u> *absolutely dreadful.*
<u>The Prado Museum is</u> *absolutely wonderful.*

1. .... absolutely dreadful.
2. .... absolutely wonderful.
3. .... absolutely boiling.
4. .... absolutely incredible.
5. .... absolutely enormous.
6. .... absolutely furious.

B ☐☐ Listen to the intonation in the examples on the recording, and try to imitate it. In small groups, say your own sentences to each other using appropriate intonation.

2 What a memory! | vocabulary |

Take five minutes to look through the whole of Unit 12 once more.
Then just look at this page, and with a partner, write down any words or phrases you can remember from the unit on these topics:

1. Things people own but don't often use
   Example: *a barbecue*
2. Places where people store things
   Example: *in a store cupboard*
3. Words relating to water
   Example: *ocean*
4. Free gifts you get on flights
   Example: *a flannel*
5. Words you can use with *absolutely*
   Example: *absolutely furious*

When you have finished, compare your words with those in the unit.

REVIEW OF UNIT 13

1 More crimes `vocabulary`

A Put these words into the correct columns. Use a dictionary if necessary:

shoplifting   robbery   burglary   arson   blackmail   vandalism
kidnapping   murder   smuggling   hijacking

Crime against people
murder

Crime against property
burglary

B Can you name the person who commits these crimes?

Example: *murder – a murderer*

2 What kind of citizen are you? `if sentences`

A Complete the questionnaire using a suitable verb form. Don't answer the questions yet.

WHAT KIND OF CITIZEN ARE YOU?

1
If you .... (find) $100 in the street, would you ...
☐ take it to the police station?   ☐ keep it?
☐ give it to someone who needed it?

2
If you .... (see) an old lady shoplifting in a supermarket, would you ...
☐ tell a shop assistant?   ☐ tell the woman to put it back?
☐ do nothing?

3
If you .... (be) at a bus stop and a car .... (park) there illegally, would you ...
☐ take the car number and tell a policeman?
☐ ask the driver to move the car?   ☐ ignore it?

4
If you .... (see) your neighbour hitting their dog on several occasions, would you ...
☐ tell him to stop?   ☐ do nothing?
☐ report him to the police or an animal welfare group?

5
If you .... (drive) past an empty car and scratched it by mistake, would you ...
☐ stop and look for the owner?
☐ leave a note on the windscreen with your name and phone number?
☐ drive on and do nothing?

Now work in small groups and discuss your answers to the questionnaire. Explain your reasons to each other.

B Write one more question with three possible answers as in the questionnaire. Then pass it to another group to discuss.

LOVE THY NEIGHBOUR

Language focus:	Vocabulary:
verb patterns	guessing words in context
present perfect simple and continuous	reporting verbs
	relationships

ACTS OF RANDOM KINDNESS
verb patterns; guessing words in context

1 Have you ever done any of these things? If so, when?
Discuss in small groups.

- asked a bus driver to wait for a person who was running for the bus
- pushed a stranger's car when it had broken down
- shared your umbrella with someone when it was raining
- helped a mother carry a pushchair down some stairs
- given a stranger a lift in your car on a rainy day or night
- thanked a bus or taxi driver for driving you carefully

2 Make sure you understand the word *random*, then read the text below without a dictionary. What's your opinion of the idea in the article?

WHY NOT COMMIT AN ACT OF RANDOM KINDNESS TODAY?

A new trend has started in America – random acts of kindness. Some people hope that the craze will be the answer to the violence carried out every day on the streets of their cities.

5   Basically, followers of the movement, called 'The Kindness Revolution', 'wilfully and willingly' commit 'senseless acts of beauty'.

They have been known to put coins in a stranger's parking meter to stop it running out, to pay for
10   cinema tickets for the person behind them in the queue and to give flowers to strangers.

The craze was started by San Francisco college professor Chuck Wall.

He says, 'One day the TV news reported yet
15   another random act of violence. I decided that if the word "violence" was changed to "kindness", the whole tone of the statement would be changed from negative to positive.'

A book, *Random Acts of Kindness*, has sold
20   200,000 copies. Co-author Daphne Kingma says, 'Random acts of kindness are those little sweet, lovely things you do for no reason except to be a nicer person.'

'When you do something nice for someone else,
25   it makes you and them feel better. Everyone should try it.'

The book is packed with ideas and examples of kind acts you can try:

30   ▪ Put a shopping trolley back in the right place outside the supermarket.

▪ Write to the boss of someone who has helped you, praising their employee.

35   ▪ Smile and wave to someone trying to push in front of you in traffic.

▪ Let the person behind you in the supermarket queue go first.

▪ Give another driver your parking
40   spot.

▪ Carry a Polaroid camera and take people's pictures for them.

▪ Take a pot plant to your local hospital, police or fire station.

45   ▪ Open your address book at random and send a greetings card to an old chum.

▪ When you are driving along an ugly road, stop and plant a tree.

50   ▪ Offer to buy a burger for the person behind you at a hamburger restaurant.

▪ Pick up litter.

▪ If you pass a beautiful garden
55   regularly, congratulate the owner on producing such a wonderful display.

▪ Smile at strangers.

▪ If you are the boss, bring your secretary a cup of coffee.

60   ▪ Buy a bag of sweets at the cinema, take one and pass it down the row.

Exchange your opinions in groups.

3 Work with a partner. Can you explain the meaning of these words as they appear in the text? Compare your answers with another pair.

craze (line 3)   running out (line 9)   packed with (line 27)
praising (line 33)   chum (line 47)   row (line 61)

4 Look at all the acts of kindness again. Which do you think are ...

– real acts of kindness?
– not especially kind?
– a bit silly?

Discuss in groups.

5 Some verbs in this table are usually associated with acts of kindness; others usually have a more negative meaning. Rewrite them in two columns, one positive and one negative.

verb + infinitive	*verb + object* *+ preposition*★	*verb + object + infinitive* *without* to
promise to do something threaten to do something offer to do something refuse to do something agree to do something	prevent somebody from doing something thank somebody for blame somebody for congratulate somebody on accuse somebody of praise somebody for	make somebody do something let somebody do something help somebody (to) do something

★ remember that when a verb follows a preposition, you use an *-ing* form, e.g. *I thanked her for writing to me.*

Compare your lists with a partner.

6 Write down your own ideas for acts of kindness, using the verbs in the positive column.

Example: *promise to help my partner with their homework.*

Tell your ideas to the rest of the group and see what they think of them.

NEIGHBOURS   present perfect simple and continuous

1 Read the sentences in the table.
✓ means correct and ✗ means incorrect.

I've lived here for about two years. ✓	I've been living here for about two years. ✓
I've known him for five years. ✓	I've been knowing him for five years. ✗
I've read your book. ✓	I've been reading your book. ✓ (but with a different meaning)
A: You look tired. B: Yes, I've painted the living room. ✗	A: You look tired. B: Yes, I've been painting the living room. ✓

With a partner, can you explain ...

– what tenses are being used?
– why some sentences are right, and some are wrong?
– what the different sentences mean?

2 ▭ Listen to the teacher on the recording talking about the sentences in Exercise 1. Make notes about each pair of sentences, and then compare your notes with your partner.

3 Get out of this maze. Work with a partner. Begin at the START sentence. If you think the sentence is correct, follow the black arrow to the next number (4). If you think it is incorrect, follow the red arrow to (3). Then decide about this new sentence. You will get out of the maze if you visit *all* the numbers once and make the right decisions. So keep a list of the numbers as you visit them.

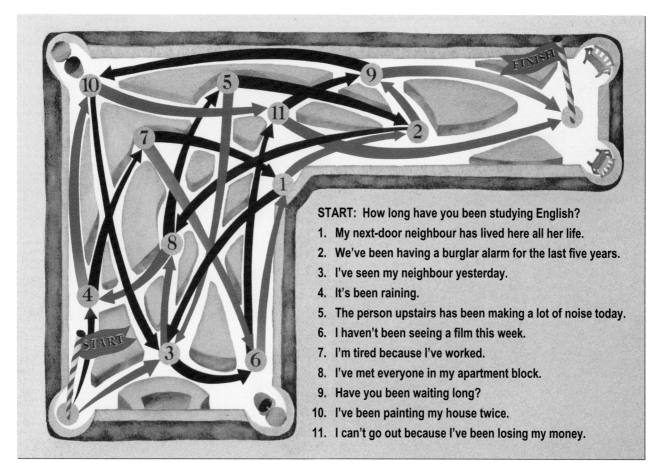

START: How long have you been studying English?
1. My next-door neighbour has lived here all her life.
2. We've been having a burglar alarm for the last five years.
3. I've seen my neighbour yesterday.
4. It's been raining.
5. The person upstairs has been making a lot of noise today.
6. I haven't been seeing a film this week.
7. I'm tired because I've worked.
8. I've met everyone in my apartment block.
9. Have you been waiting long?
10. I've been painting my house twice.
11. I can't go out because I've been losing my money.

4 Work with a partner. One of you should read the text on this page, while the other reads the text on page 172. Then close your books and tell each other:

1. what the problem is;
2. how long it has been going on;
3. any special things that have happened.

Hospital worker Pat Fisher is at her wit's end. For eighteen years her next-door neighbour has been playing loud rock music almost every night. She has complained to the police and local authorities but neither has been able to stop the noise. Pat even tried to sell the house, but interested buyers changed their minds when they heard the noise from next door. 'I'm trapped here and I'm desperate,' says Pat.

5 Discuss these questions in small groups.

1. Do you think Pat and Norman's problems could happen where you live?
2. What would you do if you were in their situation?
3. Can you think of any other noises that neighbours make that can be annoying?
4. What other kinds of problems do people sometimes have with their neighbours? Do you know anyone who has had personal experience of problems like these?

1 There are many different groups in society. Can you add one more group to this list?

- the family group
- friendship groups
- work teams/groups
- sports teams/groups
- religious/church groups
- neighbourhood groups
- leisure groups, e.g. walking or cycling, etc.

Which of these groups do you belong to, or have you belonged to?

2 Use a dictionary to check that you understand the underlined words and phrases in these sentences. Then decide which sentences are features of *good* groups.

1. People <u>get on well with</u> each other.
2. They <u>have rows</u> all the time.
3. They <u>get on each other's nerves</u>.
4. They are prepared to <u>compromise</u>.
5. They feel they <u>have something in common</u>.
6. They <u>trust</u> each other.
7. New members of the group <u>fit in</u> easily.
8. People work hard to <u>create conflict</u>.
9. People are <u>tolerant</u> towards each other.
10. The <u>atmosphere</u> among the group is <u>supportive</u>.
11. There is a lot of <u>hostility</u> in personal <u>relationships</u>.

Compare your answers in small groups.
Can you change the other sentences to make them features of *good* groups?

3 Think about one group from Exercise 1 that you are in (e.g. your family, or a friendship group). Are the sentences above true of that group or not? Give examples where possible.

Example: *In my group at work, we get on well with each other most of the time. Sometimes people have rows, but they don't last long and they aren't very important. There is one person who gets on my nerves, but that is all …*

4 〔CD〕〔CD〕 Listen to the people on the recording talking about groups they have been in, and complete the table.

	Type of group	Positive features	Negative features
Speaker 1	....	....	....
Speaker 2	....	....	....

5 Work in small groups. You are going to set up a special group of your own.

Examples: *Fans or supporters of a team, a music band or an orchestra.*
A society for the protection or preservation of something.
A charity.

Decide what the group is, then write down ...

– the name of the group.
– two or three aims of the group.
– how and where you might publicise it to get new members.

Present your ideas to the class, and see if you can sign up any new group members.

PERSONAL STUDY WORKBOOK

In your Personal Study Workbook, you will find more exercises to help you with your learning. For Unit 15, these include:

- an exercise to test yourself on the present perfect simple and continuous
- several vocabulary exercises
- an exercise on sounds and spelling
- a surprising text about the company wolves keep
- an opportunity for you to write about your neighbourhood

REVIEW AND DEVELOPMENT

REVIEW OF UNIT 13

1 Dancing with thieves? | listening and discussion |

A What possible link could there be between criminals and ballet dancing? In small groups, think of two different links, then tell the class.

B 〔CD〕 Listen to the recording. What does it tell you about criminals and ballet dancing? Make notes.

C What's your opinion? Discuss in groups.

2 Who does what? vocabulary: who as subject

A Answer these questions with a partner.

Example *Who commits crimes?*
          Criminals do.

1. Who steals from people's houses?
2. Who arrests people?
3. Who suffers because of crimes against them?
4. Who goes on trial?
5. Who defends people in court?
6. Who gives evidence in court?
7. Who decides if a criminal is innocent or guilty?
8. Who sentences people?

Tell your partner to shut their book and test them on these questions.

B Look at the answers below and write questions for them. If you like, make them funny. Remember that *who* is the subject of the questions, so you don't need an auxiliary.

1. ....? Hairdressers do.
2. ....? Actors do.
3. ....? Politicians do.
4. ....? Dentists do.
5. ....? Authors do.
6. ....? Mechanics do.

Ask your questions in mixed order in groups. Can other people give the correct answer?

REVIEW OF UNIT 14

1 Tower block incident narrative tenses

Work with a partner. Link these pictures into a story. Make sure you include at least one example of the past continuous, and one of the past perfect. Tell your story to another pair.

2 Listen and answer vocabulary

📼 Listen to the recording and and answer each question with *yes* or *no*. Check your answers with Tapescript 2 on page 174.
Read the sentences again to a partner and see if they can answer correctly.

YES AND NO

Language focus:
saying *no* politely
forming negatives
something, anything, nothing
if sentences with *would* and *might*
wish + past simple

Vocabulary:
negative prefixes
negative adverbs, e.g. *rarely*

SAYING *NO* POLITELY *if* sentences with *would* and *might*; polite refusals

1 In your country, could you say *no* in the situation below? When might it be necessary to say *no*, do you think? Discuss your answers with a partner.

Some people you don't know very well invite you to dinner at their home. For the main course, they offer you something to eat which you really hate.

2 ⬚⬚ ⬚⬚ Listen to two people from different countries talking about the same situation and make notes. Write where they come from, and whether they think it is acceptable or not to say *no*.

3 Work in small groups and discuss whether you could say *no* in these situations. Here is some language to help you:

I probably wouldn't	say *no*		because …
I might	refuse	in that situation	if …
I'd probably	say *yes*		
I definitely would(n't)	accept		

1. Imagine you had to go to your boss's house one evening to deliver some documents, and he/she invited you in for a drink. What would you do?

2. Suppose a stranger sitting near you in an airport lounge asked you to look after their suitcase for a few minutes. How would you react?

3. Imagine someone you knew quite well invited you to a party. And suppose too that they knew you weren't busy that evening. What would you do?

4. Imagine you were waiting for a friend to join you for lunch in a café, and he was late. And suppose there was a free seat at the table, and a stranger asked if they could sit there. How would you react?

5. Suppose someone came to your door collecting money for charity. What would you do?

6. Imagine a friend asked if they could use your phone. How would you respond?

As a group, choose one of the situations above and tell the class what you think.

4 Work with a partner. Choose two or three of the situations from Exercise 3 and decide how you would say *no*. Here are some suggestions:

Ways of saying no*:*
I'm afraid I …
I'd love to/like to, but …
I wish I could, but …
I'm terribly sorry, but …
That's very kind of you, but …
It's a bit difficult, I'm afraid.

Excuses:
I have to …
I'm expecting …

5 Work with a partner. Write two similar problem situations, e.g. about a friend, a colleague, a classmate, a salesperson, a neighbour or a stranger. Give your situations to another pair. See if they would answer *no*, and if so, what they would say.

NEGATIVES AND OPPOSITES!

1 Write down some questions people have asked you today where you answered *yes* or *no*. Then write the name of the person who asked you.

Example: *Have you got the agenda for the meeting? (my boss)*
Is your mother coming over this evening? (my husband)
Do you want ice in it? (a barman)

Tell your partner, and tell them what you answered. Do you regret any answers?

Unit 16 YES AND NO

2 Do the quiz with a partner, then find out your score at the bottom of the page.

So you think you know your negatives?

1 Make these sentences negative. More than one answer may be possible.

- We had a very good holiday.
- Elizabeth advised me to take the job.
- I think it's raining.
- I hope so.
- He'll probably make a boring speech.
- We used to go there.

2 Use words from the table to complete the sentences.

every	some	any	no/none
everyone/	someone/	anyone/	no one/
everybody	somebody	anybody	nobody
everything	something	anything	nothing
everywhere	somewhere	anywhere	nowhere

1. I looked for hours but I couldn't find it
   . . . .
2. There's . . . . to do here; it's so boring.
3. I'm sure there must be . . . . who can help.
4. She took . . . . out of the fridge and then put it all back.
5. Are you saying there isn't . . . . you can do about it?
6. I don't want to see him . . . . more.
7. There's . . . . chance of success, I'm afraid.

3 What is the opposite of these words? Some can take a prefix, others can't.

Example: *like*: opposite = *dislike*
           cruel: opposite = *kind*

agree	accept	admit	honest
approve	satisfied	obedient	innocent

4 Look at the four adverbs in the box. Which is the odd one out and why?

She was
rarely
invariably
seldom
hardly ever
late for work.

5 Some of these sentences are incorrect. Find the mistakes and correct them.

- Everybody have to arrive on time.
- There was nothing left.
- Neither of us have been to Italy but we can both speak Italian.
- No one tell him what to do.

6 Look at this question and answer.

Q: Do you mind if I open the window?
A: No, not at all.

Does this answer mean
    'Yes, you can open it.' or 'No, you can't.'?

Look at this dialogue.

A: I don't like chocolate.
B: Neither do I.

Does B like chocolate?

SCORE

One mark for each correct answer (total = 28):
    22 or more: Excellent
        18–21: Good
        14–17: Not bad
    less than 14: Oh dear!

---

3 Work in small groups. Complete these sentences about your classroom and the people in it. Be amusing, not cruel! Choose your best sentences to read to the class.

Example: *Nobody* has read all the works of Shakespeare in English (except possibly Julio).

1. Nobody . . . .
2. We hardly ever . . . .
3. There is someone . . . .
4. None of us . . . .
5. There is definitely nothing . . . .
6. There's no . . . .

1 These people are all in *negative* situations. They would like their situation to be different. Notice the structures with *wish*.

It's so hot in this office. I wish we had air-conditioning.

Why are the buses always late? I wish I could drive.

Another day at the office … I wish I didn't have to go to work.

1. What tense follows *wish* in the examples above?
2. What *time* are they referring to?

Look at these three people. How would they like their situation to be different?
Complete the bubbles with a partner using *wish* + past simple.

That's beautiful. I wish ....
....
....

Oh, this sun is making my eyes hurt.
I wish ....
....

It's only Tuesday – this week seems so long! I wish
....
....

2 Make a list of some of the negative thoughts you have during a normal day, and then compare in groups. Are any very common?

Examples: *I wish I could spend less time travelling to work.*
Why does nobody ever write letters to me?
I wish I had more time to relax.

3 Vera Peiffer has written a book about positive thinking. She says people need to stop thinking negative thoughts and replace them with positive ones.
Read the examples she gives.

Positive Thinking

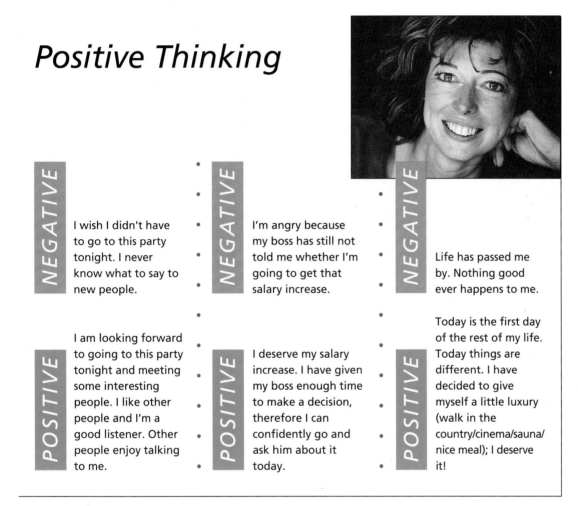

NEGATIVE
I wish I didn't have to go to this party tonight. I never know what to say to new people.

NEGATIVE
I'm angry because my boss has still not told me whether I'm going to get that salary increase.

NEGATIVE
Life has passed me by. Nothing good ever happens to me.

POSITIVE
I am looking forward to going to this party tonight and meeting some interesting people. I like other people and I'm a good listener. Other people enjoy talking to me.

POSITIVE
I deserve my salary increase. I have given my boss enough time to make a decision, therefore I can confidently go and ask him about it today.

POSITIVE
Today is the first day of the rest of my life. Today things are different. I have decided to give myself a little luxury (walk in the country/cinema/sauna/ nice meal); I deserve it!

4 Work with a partner. Write positive thoughts to replace these negative ones.

Negative
'I'm exhausted. I wish I could sit down and relax, but I can't because I still have to do the washing up.'

Positive

....

Negative
'I wish I didn't have to give a presentation at work next week. Everyone will be watching and I'll be terribly nervous.'

Positive

....
....

Now go back to the negative thoughts you wrote down in Exercise 2, and write positive thoughts. Show them to your partner.

5 Discuss in groups.

1. Do you think Vera Peiffer's ideas are useful or not?
2. Have you ever tried this technique or would you like to try it?
3. Can you think of any situations where it would be particularly helpful or unhelpful?

PERSONAL STUDY WORKBOOK

In your Personal Study Workbook, you will find more exercises to help you with your learning. For Unit 16, these include:

- negatives, negative prefixes and suffixes
- a reading passage on cultural differences in indicating *yes* and *no*
- *wish* + past simple, and *so* and *neither*
- practice in refusing invitations politely
- another page of your visual dictionary to complete – word relationships

---

REVIEW AND DEVELOPMENT

REVIEW OF UNIT 14

1 Can you hear the difference?   pronunciation

Listen to the recording. Which sentence do you hear?

1. She broke it.
   She'd broken it.
2. When I arrived he left.
   When I arrived he'd left.
3. He hasn't been before.
   He hadn't been before.
4. I was angry because she lost it.
   I was angry because she'd lost it.
5. They met a man who lived there.
   They met a man who'd lived there.
6. She injured her ankle; that's the problem.
   She'd injured her ankle; that was the problem.
7. I hope she's gone.
   I hoped she'd gone.
8. We did it because he asked us to.
   We did it because he'd asked us to.

Practise with a partner. Read one of the sentences for each number. Can your partner identify the sentence you are reading?

2 She couldn't go to school because ...   reading and writing

Read these notes sent by parents to teachers explaining why their children were absent, late or unable to do something. Which do you think are funny?

> Sorry Jimmy is late this morning. He hurt his neck and I overslept as well.

> Eric was absent this morning as he was extremely sick after breakfast.
> P.S. I am not a very good cook yet.

> Tommy and his sister were absent from school as they were suffering from conjunctivitis. I kept them off for a couple of days to keep an eye on them.

> Please excuse Bobby for being late. We had a very big dinner today.

> I'm sorry Pauline is late but she had toothache this morning. I told her she would have to go to the dentist, but she seems to be alright now.

With a partner, write three interesting, unusual or humorous notes to explain why you were absent from school or late. Show your notes to another pair.

REVIEW OF UNIT 15

1 Someone I get on well with `vocabulary`

Complete the column on the right with the name of someone you know and/or their relationship to you. Try not to repeat a name.

Example: *someone I get on with very well* Monica (my cousin)

	Names/Relationships
someone I get on with very well	....
someone I really trust	....
someone I occasionally have rows with	....
someone I have a lot in common with	....
someone from my neighbourhood I see regularly	....
someone who is very tolerant	....
someone who gets on my nerves	....
someone who I find supportive	....

Tell a partner who these people are, like this:

Example: *I get on well with Monica – she's my cousin. We live near each other and go out together a lot. She's very good company.*

2 Good and bad neighbours `tense review`

Complete the story using the verbs in brackets in the correct tense. Then compare your answers with a partner.

The Carter family .... (move) to Bristol in 1993 and they ....
.... (live) in a state of terror ever since.
The problem .... (start) soon after they .... (arrive), when a group of
animal lovers .... (buy) the house next door to them. One day, while Mr Carter
.... (work) in the garden, he .... (realise) that a tiger ....
(watch) him very attentively from the living room window of the house next door. He then
.... (notice) that someone .... (leave) the window slightly open,
so he .... (hurry) round the front to complain. His neighbours
just .... (laugh) at him. Not surprisingly, he .... (complain) to his council,
who .... (tell) him that they .... (have) problems before with these
people in their previous home.
However, things .... (get) worse when the neighbours .... (bring) home
creatures like bats, snakes, wolves and even a llama.
The Carters .... (write) at least ten times to the council to no avail, and
recently they .... (think) of moving away.

17

PACKAGING

Language focus:	Vocabulary:
partitives	holiday arrangements
numbers and quantities	prices and costs
making associations	abstract nouns

SACKS AND BARRELS   partitives and numbers

1 Match the words and pictures. Compare with a partner.

sack	carton	barrel	tube	bag	box	bucket	can/tin	jar
packet	bottle	jug	bowl	tub	mug			

2 With your partner think of two things each one could contain. Use a bilingual dictionary if necessary.

Example: *A sack could contain potatoes or coal.*

3  Listen to the people on the recording discussing what they need to buy or borrow. Complete the list below, including any quantities you hear. Then compare with a partner.

Shopping list

.... fruit juice
.... wine
.... mineral water
.... and some fizzy drinks

a couple of kilos of sausages and chicken legs
a large jar of mustard
a bottle of ketchup
a few large bags of crisps and peanuts
....bread
....
....

a tube of glue
a ball of string
....

TO BORROW...
glasses   cutlery   plates   ....

4 Write these quantities on the line below.

a few   a couple of   half a dozen   hundreds of   several   one or two
loads of   a dozen   plenty of

the least _____ the most

5 Discuss in small groups.

1. What do you think the people in the recording are buying the goods for?
2. If you had a similar event in your country, would you need the same things or different things? Tell your group what you would need.
3. Make a list of anything the people in the recording have forgotten.

6 After the event is over, what rubbish will there be? Work in pairs and complete the table, referring back to the shopping list.

Containers that can be reused	Containers that have to be thrown away
bottles	juice cartons

1 When a company is selling a new product, the brand name is very important because a name has a lot of associations. Read the two examples. Do you agree with the associations in the text? Discuss with a partner.

A vodka called 'Rasputin' immediately makes people think of images of Russia on the brink of revolution, of power, sex, mystery and so on. An advertising campaign to launch 'Rasputin' would have to focus on one or more of these associations.

A good name will give a clear picture of the 'personality' of the product. A cosmetics range called 'Loren' communicates 'graceful glamour' for the older woman. Here the reference to Italian movie actress Sophia Loren gives a distinctive set of associations.

2 Work with a partner. Check that you understand and can pronounce these words.

speed	elegance	grace	glamour	power	mystery	simplicity
status	luxury	comfort	warmth	security	danger	sex appeal

3 Discuss the suggestions for brand names on the left, using the phrases on the right, words from Exercise 2, and your own associations.

1. a car called *Eagle*
2. a magazine for men called *21* and for women called *Homelife*
3. an aftershave called *Rocky* and a perfume called *Princess*
4. a hotel called *Paradise Park*
5. a chocolate bar called *Heaven*

It makes me think of (comfort)
I associate it with (warmth and security)
I tend to think of (danger)

4 Look at the Cognac advertisement. In small groups, discuss the following:

1. What associations do you have with the words and pictures?
2. What do you think is good about the advertisement?
3. Are there any things you don't like about it?

"After five hours talking, Messieurs Picasso and Braque separated on the most cordial of terms."
Montparnasse, 1907.

Salignac. Grande Fine Cognac.

5 🎧 Listen to the advertising expert on the recording. Write down any points you didn't discuss in Exercise 4.

Compare your answers in groups, then think of your own product and choose a name for it. What do others think?

1 Have you ever been on *a package holiday*?
If so, where and when? What was it like?
If not, why not?
Would you consider going on one?
Discuss in small groups.

2 What is usually included in the price of the holiday? In your groups, add to this list:

1. The accommodation is included.

3 Package holidays don't necessarily cover *all* the costs.

Read the checklist and tick (✓) the questions and underline the words which refer directly to costs/expenses. Compare with a partner.

① Are any of the following <u>covered</u>, or will you have to pay extra?
  a. On the journey
     for weekend or day flights
     for airport or port taxes, security charges
     for transfer between airport or port and hotel
  b. At the hotel
     for full board/half board
     for a single room
     for a balcony/view/special room
     for a private toilet/shower/bath

② How much do you pay for insurance?

③ What is the cost of travel from your home to the airport/port?

④ Are there price reductions or free holidays for children?

⑤ What do the booking conditions say about surcharges because of fuel price increases or changes in the exchange rate?

⑥ Will any excursions or entertainment be included?

⑦ What meals are provided on the journey?

⑧ How far is the hotel from local shops or entertainments?

⑨ Does it have facilities for children like special meal times, babysitters and a games room?

⑩ Are the beaches suitable for bathing, especially for children?

YOUR HOLIDAY CHECKLIST

4 Work with a partner. For each of these questions, think of another example in a different context.

Example: *Is .... included?*
(in a school) Is the price of textbooks included in the fees?

1. Is ...... included?
2. Is there any reduction for ....?
3. Is/Are ...... covered in the total cost?
4. Is/Are .... provided?
5. Are there facilities for ......?
6. Is/Are .... suitable for ....?

Find a new partner. Tell them your questions. Can they say which context you chose?

5 Work with a partner. One of you is going to be a customer, the other a travel agent. Read the holiday advertisement, then look at your instructions.

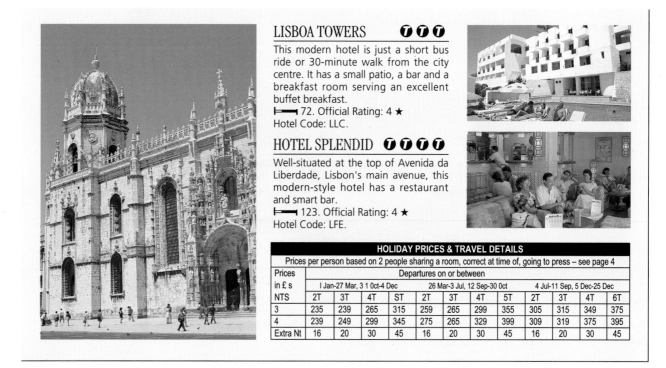

LISBOA TOWERS 🛏🛏🛏
This modern hotel is just a short bus ride or 30-minute walk from the city centre. It has a small patio, a bar and a breakfast room serving an excellent buffet breakfast.
🛏 72. Official Rating: 4 ★
Hotel Code: LLC.

HOTEL SPLENDID 🛏🛏🛏🛏
Well-situated at the top of Avenida da Liberdade, Lisbon's main avenue, this modern-style hotel has a restaurant and smart bar.
🛏 123. Official Rating: 4 ★
Hotel Code: LFE.

HOLIDAY PRICES & TRAVEL DETAILS											
Prices per person based on 2 people sharing a room, correct at time of, going to press – see page 4											
Prices in £ s	Departures on or between										
NTS	I Jan-27 Mar, 3 1 Oct-4 Dec				26 Mar-3 Jul, 12 Sep-30 Oct				4 Jul-11 Sep, 5 Dec-25 Dec			
	2T	3T	4T	ST	2T	3T	4T	5T	2T	3T	4T	6T
3	235	239	265	315	259	265	299	355	305	315	349	375
4	239	249	299	345	275	265	329	399	309	319	375	395
Extra Nt	16	20	30	45	16	20	30	45	16	20	30	45

TRAVEL AGENT
Look at the advertisement for Lisbon, and then study the Holiday Information on page 173. Be prepared to answer any questions on package tours to Lisbon.

CUSTOMER
Choose one of the role cards below, read the advertisement carefully, and then look back at your Holiday Checklist in Exercise 3. Does the advertisement answer these questions, and any others you want to ask? If not, get answers from the travel agent.

ROLE CARDS

---

1 You are planning a four-night stay in Lisbon with a friend. You are interested in excursions, and you want to know if it is possible to book them now. You have also been warned about 'hidden costs', so you want to know exactly what the holiday will cost.

---

2 You are planning a five-night stay in Lisbon with your wife/husband and ten-year-old son. You would like to know about any reductions for children, and what would happen if you wanted to change the date of your departure at short notice.

Unit 17 PACKAGING

REVIEW AND DEVELOPMENT

REVIEW OF UNIT 15

1 Thank you for helping me   reporting verbs

Which of the following have you done this week ...

- thanked someone for doing something?
- blamed someone for something?
- congratulated someone on doing something?
- threatened to do something?
- accused someone of doing something?
- made someone do something?
- refused to do something?
- offered to do something?

Think of specific examples. Then work in small groups, and tell each other about them.

Example: *Someone in my apartment block asked me to help him push his car. I had to refuse to do it because I've got a bad back.*

2 You look hot   present perfect continuous

Think of suitable responses to these questions or statements, and then practise the dialogues with a partner. Use a dictionary to help you if necessary.

Example: A: *Why are your hands yellow?*
B: *Well, I've been painting the kitchen, and I usually end up with more on my hands than the wall.*

1. Why are you sweating so much?
2. Your hands are filthy.
3. You look tired.
4. Why do you smell of onion?
5. Your face is very red. Is it burnt?
6. Why are your shoes so muddy?
7. Your English is much better now.
8. You look bored.

REVIEW OF UNIT 16

1 The yes/no game   listening and speaking

A 🔲 Listen to the people
on the recording playing a game.
When you hear a funny noise,
the person answering the
questions has lost. What do you
think the rules of the game are?

B 🔲 Listen to the second contestant again. Write down all her answers. Why does she lose?

C It's your turn. Work with a partner. Write a list of yes/no questions to start you off with the game, like this:

1. Can you speak English?
2. Are you going out tonight?
3. You didn't come to class yesterday, did you?

Form groups of three or four. Play the game as on the recording. Each player has to keep going for 60 seconds to win.

2 How many people can speak English here?   indefinite pronouns

Work with a partner. Write questions which will produce answers with the words in the box (and no other words).

Example: *How many people in this class have beards?* (None)
          Who can write a letter to the newspapers? (Anybody)

nothing	anything	everywhere	none	somebody	anybody
nowhere	everything	anywhere			

Find a new partner. Ask them your questions, and see if they use the correct word from the box.

18

HONESTLY SPEAKING

Language focus:	Vocabulary:
reported speech	reporting verbs
reported questions	politics and economics
	triumphs and disasters

1 Read the conversations in the pictures. What tense changes do you notice? What is the reason for the changes?

2 Now complete the rest of the tense changes in the box and compare your answers with a partner.

Direct speech	Reported speech
'I'm going out.'	He said (that) he .... going out.
'They work in Rome.'	She told me (that) they .... in Rome.
'We don't know him.'	They told us (that) they .... him.
'I found the letter.'	He told her (that) he .... the letter.
'She's lost her wallet.'	He said (that) she .... her wallet.
'I can't remember.'	She told him (that) she .... remember.
'You must pay the fees before Friday.'	He said (that) I .... pay the fees before Friday.

3 Think of three or four things people said or told you earlier today. Write them down. Then compare your answers in groups. Are there any unusual sentences?

Examples: *My wife said she was going out tonight.*
A stranger in the street told me I had dropped my glove.
My son said he loved me.

When you have finished, look at the Grammar Reference on page 168 for more details about reported speech.

4 🎧 Dorothy Parker (1893–1967) was an American humorist and writer. The extract below is from the beginning of a short story called *A Telephone Call*.

Listen to the recording and follow the extract at the same time. Then think of three adjectives to describe the character of the speaker. Compare with your partner.

Please, God, let him telephone me now. Dear God, let him call me now. I won't ask anything else of you, truly I won't. It isn't very much to ask. It would be so little to you, God, such a little, little thing. Only let him telephone now. Please, God, please, please, please. If I didn't think about it, maybe the telephone might ring. Sometimes it does that. If I could think of something else. If I could think of something else. Maybe if I counted five hundred by fives, it might ring by that time. I'll count slowly. I won't cheat. And if it rings when I get to three hundred, I won't stop; I won't answer it until I get to five hundred. Five, ten, fifteen, twenty, twenty-five, thirty, thirty-five, forty, forty-five, fifty ... Oh, please let it ring. Please. This is the last time I'll look at the clock. I will not look at it again. It's ten minutes past seven. He said he would telephone at five o'clock. 'I'll call you at five, darling.' I think that's where he said 'darling'. I'm almost sure he said it there. I know he called me 'darling' twice, and the other time was when he said goodbye. 'Goodbye, darling.' He was busy, and he can't say much in the office, but he called me 'darling' twice. He couldn't have minded my calling him up. I know you shouldn't keep telephoning them – I know they don't like that. When you do that, they know you are thinking about them and wanting them, and that makes them hate you. But I hadn't talked to him in three days – not in three days. And all I did was ask him how he was; it was just the way anybody might have called him up. He couldn't have minded that. He couldn't have thought I was bothering him. 'No, of course you're not,' he said. And he said he'd telephone me. He didn't have to say that. I didn't ask him to, truly I didn't. I'm sure I didn't. I don't think he would say he'd telephone me, and then just never do it. Please don't let him do that. God. Please don't. 'I'll call you at five, darling.' 'Goodbye, darling.' He was busy, he was in a hurry, and there were people around him, but he called me 'darling' twice. That's mine, that's mine. I have that, even if I never see him again.

5 Work with a partner and complete the sentence beginnings.

1. She wanted the man ....

2. The man promised ....

3. When she rang, she asked him ....

4. When she rang, he told her ....

5. She admitted ....

6. She refused to believe ....

6 📼 Listen to the recording of the actual conversation between the man and the woman. Was she being honest with herself? Discuss in groups and give reasons.

HONEST ANSWERS
reported questions

1 Work with a partner. Put the reported questions into direct speech, and then decide who asked the questions and in which context.

Reported question	Direct question	Speaker / Context
1. She asked me if I understood the grammar point.	*Do you understand the grammar point?*	*your English teacher in a lesson*
2. He asked me how long I was planning to leave my car there.	*How long are you planning to leave your car there?*	*a traffic warden or police officer in the street*
3. He asked me if I had anything to declare.		
4. She asked me if I could do overtime that evening.		
5. They asked me if I had done that kind of work before.		
6. She asked me where it hurt.		
7. He asked me why I was carrying a knife in the street.		
8. She asked me when I would be able to pay the rent.		

2 Read these rules about the grammar of reported questions. Are they true or false? Discuss with a partner.

1. When you report a question in English, you usually move the tenses 'one tense back': for example, *will* becomes *would*.
2. Reported questions end with a question mark (?).
3. In reported questions the word order is usually different from direct questions.
4. The auxiliary *do/does/did* is used in reported questions.
5. If you are reporting a *yes/no* question (Example: *Are you busy? Yes/No*), you need to put *if* after the reporting verb.

3 Would you always give honest answers to the questions you wrote in Exercise 1? Discuss in groups and give reasons.

4 With your partner, write down another possible reported question for each of the situations in Exercise 1.

Example: Situation 1: *She asked us if we had any other problems we wanted to discuss.*

Work with a new partner. Tell them the sentences you wrote (in a different order), and see if they can identify the situation and speaker.

5 As a class, think of the names of ten famous living people everyone knows. For example:

a politician   a musician   an actor/actress   an artist   a public figure
a writer   an inventor or explorer

Divide into groups of four. Each group chooses one of the famous people. Now divide each group into pairs. Make a list of five or six questions you would ask your famous person.

Example: *Why did you become an artist?*

Now interview a different person from your original group using your questions. Let them interview you too. At the end, tell someone from another group what questions you were asked and what answers you gave.

Example: *He asked me why I became an artist, and I told him it was because I had always loved painting.*

1 Work in small groups. Make a list of events that are in the news at the moment. Are there any news stories similar to the photos? Which is the most important current news story?

2 Work with a partner, and use a dictionary to check the meaning and pronunciation of the words in the list. Then divide them into the three categories in the table. Some words may go in more than one category.

flood   redundancies   election defeat   riots   famine   trade agreement
inflation rate   drought   peace talks   epidemic   industrial dispute
avalanche   trade union victory   ministerial row   foreign policy

The economy	*Politics*	*Natural disasters*
....	....	....
....	....	....
....	....	....
....	....	....
....	....	....
....	....	....

Compare your answers with another pair.

3 📖 Listen to the news headlines, and write them down. Check your answers with Tapescript 3 on page 174.

4 Work in groups and discuss these points.

1. Which of the news headlines in Exercise 3 are good news and which are bad?
2. Is the balance of good and bad news stories similar to the news reports in your country?
3. Do you think the balance is right? Should news reports have more or fewer good news stories? Why?

5 Read the text about the views of a British news journalist. Do you agree with him? Tell a partner.

No news is good news

Martyn Lewis believes that the media in Britain are obsessed with disaster and that they give a distorted view of the world. He says that TV news visits people, organisations and countries when things are going wrong for them, but rarely goes back when things start to go right. For example, a few years ago, an area of the country suffered from riots and violence and this was widely reported. But since then, through good policing and a new self-help community policy, there has been a significant decrease in crime in the area, but this has not been reported on the national news. He says that when news editors discuss the day's priorities, there should be a more representative balance of the stories that affect or change the country or the world we live in. This will give more weight to achievements and successes, so that people who watch the news are more aware of the changes that offer hope for the future. For instance, in a war report showing the disaster that is happening, the rescue of people trapped near the front line is a moving and uplifting story which needs to be shown. He feels that journalism on TV has reached a high standard. But although it must report failure and expose weakness and injustice, it must also show the accomplishments, successes and triumphs so that viewers get a balanced and fair picture of the world.

6 Look at the text again and underline words which express the good news idea. The first has been done for you.

PERSONAL STUDY WORKBOOK

In your Personal Study Workbook, you will find more exercises to help you with your learning. For Unit 18, these include:

- exercises on reported speech, reported questions and reporting verbs
- an exercise on political vocabulary
- listening and reading texts in which speakers talk about telling lies
- writing an informal letter

REVIEW OF UNIT 16

1 Find someone who ... | questions and negatives |

Work with a partner. You have to find other people in the class for whom the sentences below are true. First, write out the most logical questions to ask for each sentence.

Example: *What did you have for breakfast this morning?*
or *Did you have anything to eat for breakfast this morning?*

Find someone who ... Name

– had nothing to eat for breakfast ....
– hardly ever thinks about the past ....
– hasn't been anywhere interesting this week ....
– rarely speaks English outside the class ....
– has done none of the Personal Study Workbook exercises for this unit ....
– eats everything they are given ....
– has no time to themselves ....
– probably won't go to bed before midnight tonight ....

Check the questions with your teacher before you move around the class to find the answers.

2 It's a question, isn't it? | pronunciation |

A Here are some examples of question tags:

He lives in Madrid, *doesn't he*?
You didn't see the others, *did you*?
They're coming this evening, *aren't they*?
It's a big place, *isn't it*?
You aren't married, *are you*?
You've got two brothers, *haven't you*?

When the voice rises on the question tag, it is a real question and the speaker isn't sure of the answer. When the voice falls, the speaker probably knows the answer but wants confirmation of it.

🔊 Listen to the same six questions on the recording. Which ones are real questions?

B Complete each of these with the correct question tag and compare your answers with a partner.

1. It's a beautiful town, ...?
2. You're going tonight, ...?
3. She didn't come yesterday, ...?
4. You're an architect, ...?
5. You haven't seen my pen, ...?
6. He went to the party, ...?

Say each of the questions to your partner. Go up on some of the question tags and down on others. Can your partner identify which are real questions? If you disagree, your teacher can listen and tell you if the problem is the pronunciation or the listening.

Is she asking me or telling me?

This is lovely, isn't it?

3 Positive thinking   vocabulary

Read through the list. Is your first thought for each one positive, negative, or neutral?
Write *P*, *N*, or *Neut*, next to each one.

computers   my salary   speeches   overtime   charity   success
airport lounges   luxury   queues   my boss   beards   parties
spiders   answerphones   eating liver and kidney   allergies
my workplace / place of study

Discuss your answers with other people in the class.

REVIEW OF UNIT 17

1 Bigger, smaller or the same size?   partitives

Work in small groups and discuss whether the items below are bigger, smaller or the
same size as each other.

1. a bag of rice or a sack of rice
2. a basket of fruit or a tin of fruit
3. a loaf of bread or a slice of bread
4. a mouthful of honey or a jar of honey
5. a ball of string or a piece of string
6. a jug of water or a bucket of water
7. half a dozen bottles of wine or a barrel of wine
8. a tub of ice cream or a spoonful of ice cream
9. a handful of peanuts or several peanuts
10. a packet of spaghetti or a portion of spaghetti

2 Glamour and glamorous   word building; abstract nouns

Find the abstract nouns from the mixed up letters in the column on the left. Then
complete each sentence with the correct form of the word.

WEPOR   *p o w e r*   He was a very *p o w e r f u l* leader.

CAELEGNE   _ _ _ _ _ _ _ _   1. She always looked very _ _ _ _ _ _ _.

RUXLUY   _ _ _ _ _ _   2. They lived in a large, _ _ _ _ _ _ _ _ _ home.

RHTWAM   _ _ _ _ _ _   3. I have always found him a very _ _ _ _ person.

RENADG   _ _ _ _ _ _   4. Flying is not a _ _ _ _ _ _ _ _ _ form of transport.

ROMTCOF   _ _ _ _ _ _ _   5. Always buy walking shoes that are _ _ _ _ _ _ _ _ _ _ _.

ARGEC   _ _ _ _ _   6. He was a most _ _ _ _ _ _ _ _ dancer.

LPMSIICYIT   _ _ _ _ _ _ _ _ _ _ 7. I like my life to be really _ _ _ _ _ _.

RESMYTY   _ _ _ _ _ _ _   8. He left the building and was never seen again. It was very

_ _ _ _ _ _ _ _ _.

PLAIN ENGLISH

Language focus:
formal and informal English
should, ought to and *had better*
verb + *-ing* form, preposition + *-ing* form, adjective + infinitive

Vocabulary:
bureaucracy
writing a curriculum vitae
symptoms of fear

PLAIN ENGLISH OR GOBBLEDYGOOK?
formal and informal English

1 Do you ever have to read or fill in these documents? If so, which words in the box below best describe them? Discuss with a partner.

- tax forms
- legal documents
- literature from your bank
- official government leaflets
- job application forms

clear   full of jargon   confusing   concise   complicated
straightforward   long-winded

2 An organisation in Britain was set up to improve documents giving information to the public, and make them easier to understand. Read about it and do the tasks below.

The Plain English Campaign

The Plain English Campaign was formed in 1979. Its aim was to improve the quality of English used in public information documents, so that ordinary people understood exactly what was written. Usually this meant taking out jargon and unnecessarily difficult language. In some cases the campaign has been very successful, and one example is the document published by the tax office: 'Are you paying too much tax on your savings?' This leaflet shows people on low incomes how to get tax back on their savings. In just twelve short sentences, it explains the tax position for savings, explains what action you can take and tells you how to get more information. It is supported by humorous cartoons and uses very friendly language.

Another example is the 'British Lung Foundation: The Facts'. There are ten leaflets here with titles such as 'Asthma' or 'Smoking and your lungs', and they give information about lung diseases. There are no wasted words in these leaflets, and each one breaks up the text with clear headings and helpful diagrams. All technical terms are carefully explained in simple concise English.

In contrast, here is an extract from an official document which the Plain English Campaign does not find clear or helpful.

A definition of 'hospital beds':

A device or arrangement that may be used to permit a patient to lie down when the need to do so is a consequence of the patient's condition rather than the need for active intervention such as examination, manipulative treatment, obstetric delivery or transport ...'

Based on the text, write down at least two more ways public documents can be made clear.

1. *Documents should be in everyday English.* ....
2. ....
3. ....

3 🔲🔲 Compare your points with another pair and then listen to a woman from the Plain English Campaign. Write down any other points that she mentions.

4 With a partner, rewrite these examples of formal English in simple, everyday English.

Example: *In case of fire customers are requested to leave the premises without delay.* (notice in shop)
        That means if there's a fire, you must leave the building immediately.

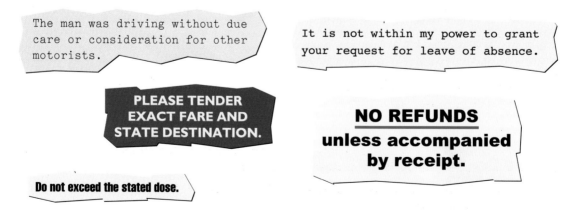

The man was driving without due care or consideration for other motorists.

It is not within my power to grant your request for leave of absence.

PLEASE TENDER EXACT FARE AND STATE DESTINATION.

NO REFUNDS unless accompanied by receipt.

Do not exceed the stated dose.

1 What is a *curriculum vitae*, and have you ever had to write one? If so, what was it for? Tell a partner.

2 Some people make terrible mistakes in their CVs and letters of application. Here are some examples. What is wrong in each case? Work with your partner.

Among his skills, one candidate included: 'excellent memory, good at mathematics, excellent memory'.

One person addressed his letter to 'Dear Sir or Modem', whilst another claimed to be a 'quick leaner'.

A secretary stated her typing ability as '756 words a minute', and another woman said that she left her previous job after 'maturity leave'.

One man concluded his letter of application: 'I look forward to hearing from you shorty.'

'I look forward to hearing from you shorty.'

Another job hunter, an accountant, produced a 43-page life story, which included a picture of his wife and children and a copy of a first-aid certificate.

Hobbies listed by applicants have included 'witchcraft, euthanasia, afghan hounds', and 'nudism'.

An American applying for a job in England gave the name of his shoeshine man as a referee. He thought it was important for a future employer to know that he took care of his shoes.

'... excellent memory, good at mathematics, excellent memory, ...'

Compare your answers with another pair.

3 What information do you think a CV ought to include, and in what order? How long should it be? Discuss in small groups.

4 ▭ The man on the recording is an experienced recruitment consultant. Listen to his advice on writing a CV and make notes. Then compare with a partner.

Do you agree with all the advice given on the recording? Is there anything the man does not say that you think he should?

5 On the recording, the man uses *ought to* and *should* with more or less the same meaning – what he thinks is right or good for people to do. Look at Tapescript 4 on page 174 and underline the examples you find, then read this explanation and do the exercise below.

Should, *ought to* and *had better* have a similar meaning if you want to give advice or an opinion about a specific problem.

You	should ought to 'd better	go and see the doctor about your eye.

We	shouldn't ought not to 'd better not	stay too long.

(*ought not to* is often avoided in spoken English.)

We <u>don't</u> use *had better* with general advice, however.

CVs	should ought to	be typed and clearly expressed.

<u>not</u>

~~CVs had better be typed.~~

With a partner, correct any errors in the sentences. (Some are correct.)

1. You really ought leave now.
2. Shouldn't we ask her first?
3. You would better take your umbrella today.
4. I don't think people had better use personal stereos on public transport.
5. You'd better not leave your car here – you might get a parking ticket.
6. I think you ought to see a specialist.
7. Don't you think you should put your date of birth here?
8. You'd better to go to the bank now; it's closing soon.

---

1 Which of these have you done? Tell your partner what happened and how you felt.

- made a speech at a wedding or a celebration
- given a presentation at work to a group of colleagues
- given a lecture or a talk on a subject you know something about
- given a short 'thank you' speech or 'good luck' speech in front of a few people
- spoken for more than a minute to the people in your English class

2 Many people have to make speeches in their jobs or in their social lives. However, even experienced speakers sit shaking with fear before they get up to speak.
Work with a partner and a dictionary, and divide the list below into two categories:

Mental symptoms of fear   Physical symptoms of fear

> your mind goes blank   you wake up sweating in the night   you blush
> you start to shake   you feel intimidated   you bite your nails or your lips
> you feel tension in your neck   you lose the thread of your argument
> you start to stammer   your mouth goes dry

Add one or two more symptoms to each category, then compare with another pair.

3 Study the lists for one minute, then shut your book and tell your group if you suffer from any of these symptoms.

4 Look at these suggestions for overcoming problems with public speaking. With your partner add your own advice in the spaces using the same sentence constructions.

Verb + *-ing*	
try …	practising in front of the mirror
	doing relaxation exercises ....
	....
avoid …	talking for too long
	....

Preposition + *-ing*	
concentrate on …	getting your point across
	....
start by …	making a plan of what you want to say
	....
reduce fear by …	breathing deeply
	....

Adjective + infinitive	
don't be afraid to …	look at your notes
	....
be prepared to …	answer questions from the audience
	....

5 Work with a partner. You are going to prepare a short talk (maximum five minutes) to give to some of your classmates in the next lesson.

1. Choose a topic each which you know something about: a hobby, how to make something, a famous person, your work, your opinion about a social problem, etc. Tell your partner what topic you have chosen.
2. With your partner, think through the kinds of things people would be interested to know about your topic.
3. Spend a few minutes together writing a plan of the talk.
4. Either with your partner or at home, try rehearsing your talk. Don't worry about making mistakes, and avoid writing out the whole talk. (If you decide to write it out, it will probably sound much less interesting.) Just concentrate on communicating your ideas.

6 In your next lesson, form small groups (or one group if your class is small). Take turns to give your talks. When you are listening to someone else's talk, think of some questions you would like to ask them at the end.

PERSONAL STUDY WORKBOOK

In your Personal Study Workbook, you will find more exercises to help you with your learning. For Unit 19, these include:

- an exercise on the vocabulary of fear
- word building and pronunciation activities
- practice of *should*, *ought to* and *had better*
- some formal letters to read
- a curriculum vitae to complete about yourself

REVIEW AND DEVELOPMENT

REVIEW OF UNIT 17

1 Does that include everything?   vocabulary: money; package holidays

Look again at the holiday checklist on page 117. Find words or expressions with the following meanings:

1. Police or military protection of an airport ....
2. A protection agreement for people in case of accidents, theft, etc. ....
3. A lower cost or discount ....
4. An extra amount of money you have to pay for something ....
5. Given or supplied ....
6. Already paid for in the total cost ....
7. Services, buildings, or equipment on offer ....
8. Good or right or appropriate for something ....

2 I've got loads of them   numbers

Work in small groups. Tell people in your group how many of the things in the pictures you have, using the language in the box.

one (or two)	a couple of	a few
several	half a dozen	a dozen
loads of	hundreds of	plenty of

Example: *I've got about half a dozen pairs of shoes.*

REVIEW OF UNIT 18

1 Honest answers to honest questions | verb patterns with reporting verbs |

Look at these
sentence patterns
and the example
below.

You can …	ask/tell someone	(not) to do something.	
	ask someone	if when/where/why, etc.	+ clause
	tell someone	(that) when/where/why	+ clause
	say	(that)	+ clause

Example: *If a friend of yours asked you to lend them a lot of money, would you …*
   a. *ask them* .to explain why they needed it? .   b. *tell them* .you didn't have any money?
   c. *say* .you never lend money to friends?

Work with a partner. One of you should complete the questions in Box A using the
sentence patterns above; the other should complete the questions in Box B. Don't
answer the questions.

BOX A   1. If your neighbour kept making a lot of noise late at night, would you:
         a. ask them ....
         b. tell them ....
         c. say ....

         2. If you were on a train in a no-smoking compartment and someone took out
            their packet of cigarettes, would you:
         a. ask them ....
         b. tell them ....
         c. say ....

BOX B   1. If someone you knew quite well told you they had stolen something, would you:
         a. ask them ....
         b. tell them ....
         c. say ....
         2. If you found a colleague at work crying, would you:
         a. ask them ....
         b. tell them ....
         c. say ....

Now interview your partner, using your questions. What do you think of their
answers?

2 Listen very carefully … | reported speech/questions |

CD Listen to some people playing a guessing game. The woman is thinking of an
object, and the others are asking her questions. Try to remember as many questions as
possible. You can listen more than once. With a partner, write down all the things they
asked her.

Examples: *Someone asked her if you could wear it.*   *Someone asked her if you would keep it indoors.*

See which pair has the highest number of accurate reported questions.

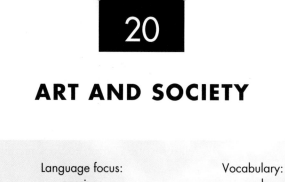

20

ART AND SOCIETY

Language focus:	Vocabulary:
passives	goods
modal passives	art and design
revision of link words	
definite, indefinite and zero article	

THE VALUE OF MONEY
passives; link words

1 How many different bank notes do you have in your currency, and do you know whose face is shown on each one? Discuss with a partner.

2 Do you know which country first used bank notes, and when? Discuss with a partner, then complete the text using words from the box.

> however   although   as a result

.... paper money was in use in China when Marco Polo visited the country in the 13th century, it was not until 1661 that the first bank note was issued in the West. Even so, until the outbreak of World War I, paper money was principally used by merchants, financiers and the rich rather than ordinary people, for whom coins were the common currency. ...., 17th- and 18th-century notes are fairly rare. ...., a considerable amount of paper money was produced in the 19th century, and some of it can still be found today. US Confederate notes and pre-revolutionary Russian notes are both highly sought after by collectors.

3 In the text in Exercise 2, how many verbs are in the active form, and how many are in the passive? Why is there such a large number in the passive? Discuss with a partner.

4 Complete the rest of the text about old bank notes. Put the verbs into the correct active or passive form.

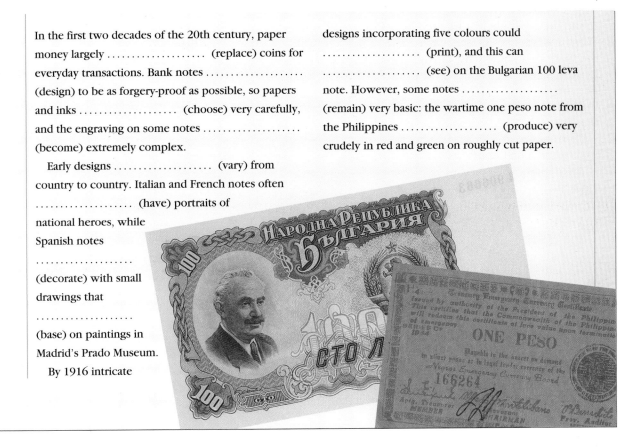

In the first two decades of the 20th century, paper money largely .... (replace) coins for everyday transactions. Bank notes .... (design) to be as forgery-proof as possible, so papers and inks .... (choose) very carefully, and the engraving on some notes .... (become) extremely complex.

Early designs .... (vary) from country to country. Italian and French notes often .... (have) portraits of national heroes, while Spanish notes .... (decorate) with small drawings that .... (base) on paintings in Madrid's Prado Museum.

By 1916 intricate designs incorporating five colours could .... (print), and this can .... (see) on the Bulgarian 100 leva note. However, some notes .... (remain) very basic: the wartime one peso note from the Philippines .... (produce) very crudely in red and green on roughly cut paper.

5 Look at other everyday things you carry. Do you like the way they are designed? Why/Why not? Can you suggest any changes? Discuss in groups.

Examples: *credit card   telephone card   driving licence   identity card   passport   transport tickets   postage stamps   cheques*

---

1 Complete these sentences about art, using one of the words in brackets to fill each gap.

1. There is .... (an exhibition/a display) of his work at the new art .... (museum/gallery) in Soho.
2. I learned to .... (draw/paint) with water colours when I was very young.
3. We need .... (an artist/a painter) to do the .... (sketches/illustrations) that go with the text in the book.
4. You can buy a .... (forgery/reproduction) of the original painting for about £50.
5. There is a .... (statue/sculpture) of Napoleon in the main square.
6. Do you know who .... (designed/drew) this cartoon?
7. Have you ever painted a self-.................... (picture/portrait)?
8. She painted .... (scenery/landscapes) and portraits.

Compare your answers with a partner.

2 ▢▢ Julia Quenzler is a court artist: in other words, she draws pictures of people in the court (including the accused) during trials. Listen to the recording about her and answer these questions.

1. In what order did these things happen?
   – she started working for the BBC[1]
   – she started her own gallery
   – she worked for NBC[2]
   – she drew people in a nightclub
2. What is the main difference between the work of a court artist in the United States and a court artist in Britain?
3. In the text, what is the significance of these times?
   – 15 minutes
   – one and a half hours
   – 15 seconds

[1] British Broadcasting Corporation
[2] National Broadcasting Corporation (America)

3 Rewrite these sentences following the first example.

1. Drawings *must be done* from memory.
   The artist *must do drawings from memory.*
2. Sketches *cannot be made* in the courtroom itself.
   The artist ....
3. People *should be drawn* accurately in court.
   The artist ....
4. Drawings *have to be produced* quickly for the television news.
   The artist ....

4 Choose one or two statements from this list that you agree with or disagree with strongly. Discuss in groups.

1. Artists should not be allowed to draw pictures in court.
2. Drawings of people on trial should be shown on television.
3. Trials should be televised.
4. Important private art collections must be opened to the public for part of the year.
5. Art galleries should not be financed with taxpayers' money.
6. The sale of paintings of national importance to overseas buyers must be approved by the government.
7. A painting was recently sold for $26 million. It is better to spend money on art than on arms.

ARTICLES AND PRECIOUS ARTICLES   vocabulary: objects; the article

1 If you could own a famous work of art such as a painting, ornament or sculpture, what would you choose, and why? Discuss your answer in groups, describing your work of art if necessary.

2 Read the text and underline all the objects you can buy in the museum shops. Compare with a partner. Are there any you would like to own?

You've seen the paintings – now buy the jewels

Art galleries are keeping debts at bay by selling replicas of objects depicted in paintings

Works of art are increasingly at the mercy of consumer tastes. Nowadays you can eat off, machine wash or put cigarette ash into
5 reproductions of some of the world's most attractive objects. In France, where this idea is particularly popular, the country's museums are currently having financial difficulties, and are
10 selling art-related accessories which allows them to pay for large exhibitions.

Take the Louvre, for instance, where you can buy reproductions of ancient
15 Egyptian and Roman jewellery and other objects. And visitors to the 1992 Toulouse-Lautrec exhibition held at the Grand Palais were able to buy disposable tablecloths decorated with
20 the artist's dancing models, a pair of long black gloves similar to those worn by a cabaret artist in a painting, and a FFr 1,200 reproduction of Lautrec's walking stick.

25 At another museum shop in the Musée d'Orsay, you can buy a pocket watch copied from the one in Alfred Stevens's *Le Bain*, a
30 copy of Cézanne's blue vase from his famous painting of the same name, and a glass and jug from a Degas painting. Keen gardeners can also
35 purchase a pair of garden shears like the ones in Manet's *Branches de pivoines blanches et sécateur*, but that seems strange, as the same tool can be found at a garden shop for a fraction of
40 the price.

But France is not alone in this craze: the shop at the British Museum in London turns over £4 million ($5.9m) and sells anything from ancient
45 Egyptian board games to terracotta figurines. In Vienna's Kunsthistorisches Museum you can buy reproduction Roman coins and plastic statues of Apollo. But in Germany most museum
50 shops must confine themselves to postcards and books, although an exception is the museum of Science and Natural History in Munich: it offers a range of educational games,
55 aeroplane kits and other toys for children of all ages.

As the barrier between art and consumerism becomes thinner, one can only hope that the art on sale in
60 the museum shops will stay as close as possible to the spirit of the original.

3 With your partner, look at the third paragraph again and discuss these questions.

1. Why is it *a pocket watch* and not *the pocket watch*? (line 27)
2. Why is it *the one in Alfred Stevens's Le Bain* and not *one in Alfred Stevens's Le Bain*? (line 28)
3. Why is it *a Degas painting* and not *the Degas painting*? (line 33)
4. Why is it *a garden shop* and not *the garden shop*? (line 39)

Together, choose ending a or b to complete the rules below:

1. We use *a/an* when we are talking about
   a. a specific example/the only one
   b. one of several/many examples

2. We use *the* when we are talking about
   a. a specific example/the only one
   b. one of several/many examples

4 Put *a/an* or *the* in the gaps.

1. I once bought .... silver necklace in .... shop in Paris.
2. .... gold necklace over there on .... table was given to me by my first husband; and by chance, he bought it in .... shop where I met my second husband.
3. I have always wanted .... nice landscape painting for .... dining room in my flat. Then last week, I found one I really liked in .... small gallery in Scotland.
4. There used to be two small bronze statues of dogs in .... middle of .... square outside my house. Then, one night, vandals stole one of .... dogs, and left .... real dog in its place. They tied .... dog to .... tree, next to .... remaining statue.

5 Look at the final paragraph again. Why is the first reference to *art* (line 57) and the second reference to *the art* (line 59)? Cross out the incorrect word in these rules.

When we want to talk about something in general,
we use / don't use *the* with a plural or uncountable noun.

When we want to talk about something particular or specific,
we use / don't use *the* with a plural or uncountable noun.

6 Complete these sentences in your own words. Then compare in small groups.

1. Museums ....
2. The museums ....
3. Jewellery ....
4. The jewellery ....
5. Money ....
6. The money ....
7. Works of art ....
8. The works of art ....

PERSONAL STUDY WORKBOOK

In your Personal Study Workbook, you will find more exercises to help you with your learning. For Unit 20, these include:

- revision of vocabulary to do with art, and work on prefixes and suffixes
- exercises to practise articles and passives
- a letter from Vincent Van Gogh to read
- recordings of people's reactions to the paintings on page 139
- another page of your visual dictionary to complete – an art gallery

---

REVIEW OF UNIT 18

1 Whatever did they ask you? | reported questions |

Look at the picture.
Write down what you think
people asked the woman. Then
compare your answers in groups.

Example: *Someone asked her where
the ladies' toilet was.*

> It's over there, next to the men's toilet.
>
> I'm afraid all flights to India are delayed this morning.
>
> I'm sorry, I've no idea why. They often don't give me any reasons!
>
> Yes, there's one upstairs and they sell all the usual basic medicines.
>
> The city centre's about 5 kilometres. You can get a bus outside the building.
>
> They run every ten minutes.
>
> No, they're shut today because it's Sunday.

2 It's the same sound | pronunciation |

The words in the boxes have
certain sounds underlined.
Match a word from Box A
which has the same <u>underlined</u>
sound in Box B.

Example: *f<u>a</u>mine* and *b<u>a</u>lance*

Compare with a partner.

Box A	Box B
f<u>a</u>mine	su<u>cce</u>ss
th<u>i</u>rd	b<u>a</u>lance
ind<u>u</u>strial	ach<u>ie</u>vement
tr<u>iu</u>mph	infl<u>a</u>tion
pol<u>i</u>ce	h<u>ur</u>t
disp<u>u</u>te	pr<u>io</u>rity
r<u>a</u>te	j<u>u</u>stice
f<u>air</u>	ref<u>u</u>se
thr<u>ea</u>ten	<u>a</u>rea

CD Listen to check your answers, then practise saying the words.

3 Politics all around you   vocabulary

Can you answer these questions about your country?

Do you know …
- the name of the political party that won the last election?
- the name of the largest trade union?
- the name of the minister responsible for foreign policy?
- the current rate of inflation?
- what percentage of the population works in agriculture?
- if there has been a serious industrial dispute recently? If so, what was it about?
- if there has been a large number of redundancies in any particular industry recently? If so, what industry?
- if your government has been involved in peace talks in any part of the world? If so, where?

REVIEW OF UNIT 19

1 Thanks for the advice   -ing form or infinitive?

With a partner, choose one of the topics in the box, then complete the sentences using the correct form (-ing or infinitive). Look back at page 133 if necessary.

> learning to skate   learning to be a comedian   learning to paint portraits
> learning to write stories for a living   learning to ski   learning to use a computer

You can start by ....

You should avoid ....

Don't be afraid ....

It's very important ....

Concentrate on ....

Try ....

You'd better be prepared ....

Tell another pair your topic and suggestions. Do they think your advice is helpful?

2 Mystery dialogues   should, ought to, had better

A Work with a partner. For each of the sentences below, think of a situation in which you might hear it, and decide who would be speaking to whom.

	Situation	Speaker/hearer
1. You ought to move that before there's an accident.	bicycle on pavement outside shop	adult to child
2. Don't you think you should put something on that?		
3. You'd better get out of here before anyone comes in.		
4. You ought to tell him before things go too far.		
5. Shouldn't you answer that?		
6. You'd better stop that or I'll get *really* angry.		
7. (should)		
8. (ought to)		
9. (had better)		

B Think of a suitable reply to each of the sentences 1–6. Tell another pair your ideas about the situations, the speakers and the replies.

C With your partner, decide on a context and write your own sentences in 7–9. Then say the sentences to another pair and see if they can guess the context you chose.

21

DARE YOURSELF TO SUCCEED

Language focus:	Vocabulary:
should have + past participle	applying for jobs
past conditional	outdoor activities
	verb/adjective + preposition

A WHITE LIE?   *should have* + past participle; job vocabulary

1 Look at the photos of two people during interviews for office jobs. Neither of them got the job. Add to the list of things they did wrong, using *should have* or *shouldn't have* + past participle.

1. She shouldn't have worn so much jewellery.

2. ....

3. ....

1. He should have trimmed his beard.

2. ....

3. ....

Compare your answers with a partner. Do you agree with their list?

2 Read the text and complete the sentences below.

DO YOU SPEAK GERMAN? NO! AND THAT'S MELANIE'S PROBLEM.

After ten years of filing and typing for the same company, Melanie was bored and depressed, so when a marketing company advertised for trainees, she applied. And when they invited her to come for an interview she was absolutely thrilled. At last, she thought, a chance to do something that would be stimulating.

There was one small problem though. Melanie hadn't been entirely honest in her application, and had told one or two white lies about her present job. Nevertheless, she dressed smartly for the interview and hoped they wouldn't discover the truth. Then half-way through, the interviewer said, 'As the advertisement stated, we are looking for someone who can speak good German.' Melanie's stomach turned. She hadn't even noticed that part of the advertisement.

'I see you studied German at school,' the interviewer went on. 'Have you kept it up?'

'Oh, yes,' nodded Melanie. 'It's like a second language to me.' She suddenly felt her face burning, but it was too late now. In fact she had studied German, but she was so awful at it that her teacher told her to give it up.

One week later Melanie was offered the job. Should she tell the truth and risk losing it? She accepted the job and said nothing.

At first it was fine. There were only three scheduled trips to Germany and other trainees volunteered to go. Meanwhile, Melanie bought some books and tapes and started learning German on her own in the evenings. It was no use though. She was still hopeless and got everything wrong.

The job itself was everything she had wanted. It was interesting and challenging and she got on well with the rest of the team. Then last week, her boss called her into his office and told her she was going to Germany on a very important trip next month. 'Pleased?' he asked. Melanie produced a weak smile. Should she come clean and tell the truth?

1. At school, Melanie .... German, but ....
....

2. The job advertisement stated that the applicants ....
.... German.

3. At the interview, Melanie said .... German.

4. When she started the job she didn't .... German.

5. In the evenings she .... German, but ....
....

6. When her boss told her she was going to Germany she realised
.... speak German.

3 Work with a partner. Write down at least three things that you believe Melanie or the interviewer should or shouldn't have done.

Example: *She should have noticed that German was necessary in the advertisement.*

Compare your sentences with another pair.

4 Work with a partner. Read the text once more if necessary, then choose *one* of these role plays and practise it together.

Role play 1. You are Melanie's friend.
She has a problem that she is very worried about. Try to encourage her to tell you what it is by asking questions:
– What's the matter?
– Why did you …?
– What are you going to …?
– When you have heard her story, give her some advice.

You are Melanie.
You are going to tell your friend about your problem at work.
When you have told her, listen to her advice, and decide what to do.

Role play 2. You are Melanie's boss.
You are very satisfied with Melanie's work, and she has made an appointment to see you about her trip to Germany. Welcome her into your office.

You are Melanie.
You have decided that the only answer is to tell your boss your secret and explain what you did and why you did it. You have an appointment to go and see him.

Act your role play for another pair. Do they think your conversation ends with a realistic solution or with good advice?

5 Discuss these questions in small groups.

1. Do you think it is acceptable to tell white lies when you are applying for a job?
2. In your country, do people normally present certificates of their qualifications when they apply for a job? If not, do you think they should?
3. Who is most responsible for Melanie's situation?

NOTHING SUCCEEDS LIKE SUCCESS   *past conditional*

1 Read the speech bubbles. Did the people succeed in what they wanted to do in each case?

1. If I hadn't wasted my time at university, I could have passed my exams.

2. If he'd panicked, the plane would have crashed.

3. We wouldn't have got the contract if I hadn't done the research.

4. I wouldn't have lost the case if I had known about the evidence.

5. We might have won the competition if we'd spent more time training.

Which speech bubble goes with the picture?

2 The sentences in the speech bubbles are all examples of the past conditional:

If + past perfect,   *would*
                       could   *have* + past participle
                       might

This form is used when people are imagining the opposite of or something different from what actually happened and are describing the consequences.
Transform these situations to express an imaginary alternative, using the past conditional.

Example: *He failed his driving test because he drove too fast.*
            If he hadn't driven so fast, he might have passed his driving test.
or   **If he had driven slower, he wouldn't have failed his driving test.**

1. She did badly in the interview and didn't get the job.
2. She came first because she worked harder than everyone else.
3. He won the card game because he cheated.
4. She didn't plan the meeting carefully and it was a terrible failure.
5. The patient lived because the operation was successful.

3 Read the text below, while your partner reads the text on page 173. Complete the last line of your text using a past conditional sentence.

A young businessman inherited a small fashion company and in a few years built up the business into a famous chain of stores. Then one evening he made a speech at a public dinner in which he joked that the clothes he sold were cheap rubbish. This comment was reported widely and in a short time, sales of his fashions fell sharply.

If ....
....

4 Close your book and tell your partner the story you read. See if they can complete it with a correct conditional sentence.

5 Think of one or two situations in your life in which you were either successful or unsuccessful. Tell your partner about them and explain how things could have been different.

Examples: *When I was a child, I did really badly in my maths exams every year. I think if someone had explained maths really clearly to me, I could have done better.*

When I was twenty-two I got a job I liked very much, working in a travel company. It meant I got a lot of opportunities to travel and see the world. I met my wife in Korea, in fact. So if I hadn't had that job, I would never have met her.

1 Read this short text and discuss your reactions in groups.

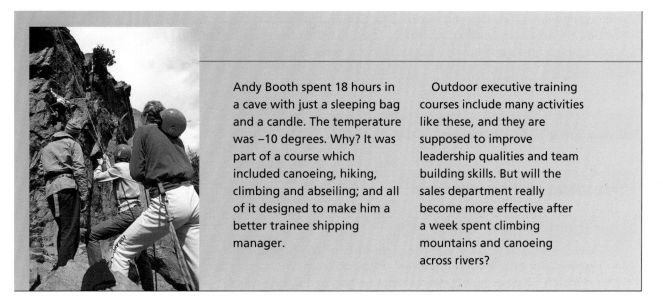

Andy Booth spent 18 hours in a cave with just a sleeping bag and a candle. The temperature was –10 degrees. Why? It was part of a course which included canoeing, hiking, climbing and abseiling; and all of it designed to make him a better trainee shipping manager.

Outdoor executive training courses include many activities like these, and they are supposed to improve leadership qualities and team building skills. But will the sales department really become more effective after a week spent climbing mountains and canoeing across rivers?

2 🎧 Now listen to four people talking about their experiences of executive training courses and complete the table.

	Opinion	Why?
1. Michael (accountant)	....	....
2. Caroline (sales team leader)	....	....
3. James (engineer)	....	....
4. Sonia (manager)	....	....

Compare your answers with a partner.

3 🎧 Listen to the first speaker on the recording again. What special problem did he have, and what would you have done in the same situation? Discuss in small groups.

4 If you were sent on an executive training course for a week, which of the things from the list below would worry you most, and why? Check any new items in a dictionary, and then discuss in groups.

sleeping in a tent
having no hot water
sleeping in a cave on your own
sharing a tent with people you work with
sailing a boat
climbing up the 10-metre mast on the boat
swimming under the boat
climbing a steep rockface
abseiling down a cliff
canoeing in a river with a strong current
building a rope bridge to get across a river
walking 20 kilometres in a day
looking foolish in front of others
the fear that you may let others down
not knowing what you may be told to do next

5 Work in groups. If you were in charge of the training budget in a large organisation, which of these would you choose for your staff? Can you add to the list?

1. Sending employees on courses designed to improve communication skills.
2. Sending employees on courses to develop their existing technical and administrative skills.
3. Sending employees on stress management or time management courses.
4. Sending employees on outdoor activity courses (like the ones described in this lesson).
5. Sending them on a short holiday so that they can relax and spend time together.
6. ....
7. ....
8. ....

Tell your group's ideas to the rest of the class.

PERSONAL STUDY WORKBOOK

In your Personal Study Workbook, you will find more exercises to help you with your learning. For Unit 21, these include:

- exercises on *should have* + past participle and the past conditional
- practice of vocabulary to do with jobs
- a text to read about how a chance meeting changed someone's life
- a letter of application to write
- another page of your visual dictionary to complete – outdoor activities

---

REVIEW AND DEVELOPMENT

REVIEW OF UNIT 19

1 British English and American English | pronunciation and vocabulary |

A British and American speakers pronounce these words differently. Can you say how?

| tomato   vase   magazine   address   hostile   inquiry   secretary   laboratory |

Listen to the recording to check your answers.

B Spelling varies too with some words. Can you provide the British English equivalent for these words?

American English	British English
color	....
labor	....
center	....
theater	....
jewelry	....
traveled	....
license (noun)	....
(bank) check	....

C The sentences below are in British English, but some of the expressions would be different in American English. Listen to the recording and write what you hear.

1. I'm visiting her tomorrow.
2. Could I speak to Albert, please?
3. I've just had some coffee.
4. I'll go and get the car.
5. half an hour
6. I can't remember if it starts at twenty to four or five past five.

2 Don't panic   `vocabulary: fear`

Find another way to express the idea in each of these sentences.

1. Your face goes red: in other words, you …
2. Your hands begin to tremble: in other words, they …
3. You can't remember what you were going to say: in other words, …
4. You desperately need to drink some water because …
5. You find it hard to speak and you keep repeating words: in other words, you …
6. Your body feels damp with fear: in other words, …

Look back at page 133 and compare your answers with a partner.

REVIEW OF UNIT 20

1 What do you think of that?   `reading and speaking`

Read the comments people made about Mark Rothko's painting, *Light Red Over Black*. Put a tick (✓) next to those who like it, and a cross (✗) next to those who don't.

1. 'I felt initial revulsion, but with time, I find it exciting.'
2. 'What you see is not quite what you get, but the idea is too simple to last a long time. I prefer more complex thought.'
3. 'An art school exercise in tone and colour. Perfectly suitable as a decoration for a gloomy restaurant.'
4. 'I enjoy the big gesture and spirit in Rothko's paintings, but I am always disappointed that I don't get the kind of spiritual experience from them that I understand others have.'
5. 'A musical painting.'
6. 'The sublime qualities disappear from Rothko's paintings as they age.'
7. 'It's too modern, it looks like a big ink splodge.'
8. 'It's one of those paintings that there is absolutely nothing to say about at all.'

Write a few sentences to express your opinion about the painting. Then compare your opinions in groups.

2 It's been stolen   `passives`

Work with a partner. Think of a suitable answer to these questions. Your answer must contain a passive construction.

Example: *What happened to the burglar?*   **He was arrested.**

1. What's happened to the money?
2. What's happening to those old buildings?
3. What happens to the theatre tickets that agencies can't sell?
4. What will happen to those old newspapers?
5. What happens to patients when they first arrive at hospital?
6. What happens to letters delivered to the wrong address?
7. What's happened to the rivers in this area?
8. What's happened to that little dog?

FORCES OF NATURE

Language focus:	Vocabulary:
used to + verb	health problems
be used to + noun or *-ing*	natural remedies
get used to + noun or *-ing*	abstract nouns
if and *unless*	word building

ONE MINUTE CHANGED OUR LIVES

be used to + noun or *-ing*

1 Organise these words into four groups, and give each group a title. Work with a partner and use dictionaries to help you.

to grab hold of something/somebody   a while   a snake   concrete   tiles
to crawl   a lizard   a squirrel   eventually   a gravestone   dawn
to last   a fortnight

Compare your groups of words with another pair and discuss any differences.

2 Look at the headline and then put the paragraphs of the story in the right order. Compare your answers with a partner.

We crawled out into utter devastation

Mary Williams and her family lost their home and most of their possessions in the 1971 Los Angeles earthquake.

☐ The rescue operations moved quite quickly, and we were all congratulated on the way we had reacted, but after about a fortnight when things began to calm down, I went into shock and for a while I could hardly talk.

☐ My first thoughts were for my daughter. It was pitch black in her bedroom and I couldn't see her, but eventually I grabbed hold of her hand and we made our way to the stairs. 'Where do we go?' I thought. I knew under the stairs was the safest place. It's human instinct to run outside, but outside the earth can swallow you up, and everything flies around – glass, tiles, and so on.

1 It was midnight on 8 February, 1971, and the children were in bed. It was a beautiful evening but unusually quiet. Normally there were hundreds of animals moving about – snakes, lizards, squirrels – but they'd all gone. I'm absolutely convinced they knew something was going to happen.

☐ When we crawled out the scene was one of utter devastation. The windows had blown out, pieces of the pavement were standing up vertically like gravestones, and glass was everywhere. Luckily none of us was seriously hurt although I had cut my hand quite badly.

☐ I came in but I couldn't relax. And when I went to bed I felt very, very uneasy. Five hours later, at 5.57am, I woke up and two things hit me simultaneously. First was the noise, which was absolutely deafening. And then there was this violent, violent shaking. I tried to grab hold of the bed but it just flew to the other side of the room. I felt for the wall; it was somehow fluid like a river.

☐ It suddenly occurred to me that I didn't know where my husband was. Then I saw him coming down the stairs. The quake had only lasted one minute and twenty-eight seconds, but it seemed like a lifetime. Like all Californian families, we had our earthquake survival kit – first aid kit, bottled water, canned food that could keep us going for 48 hours or so. We stayed under the stairs and waited for dawn.

☐ My daughter and I stayed with friends in New York and then we returned to England; but I still haven't adjusted. When you're used to picking oranges for breakfast, or going to San Francisco for a weekend, it's hard to get used to having a small house and garden in the middle of rural England. But at least these events make you respect the tremendous forces of nature. You can build marvellous cities like Los Angeles, but it only takes 6.6 on the Richter scale to reduce it all to a few bits of concrete.

3 Underline two things Mary was used to doing in California, and the thing she can't get used to in England.

4 It is easy to confuse:

> *used to* + verb
> *be used to* + noun or *-ing*
> *get used to* + noun or *-ing*

Read the three examples then complete the three definitions below.

Examples: *I found it difficult to live in England at first, because I <u>wasn't used to living</u> in such a small house.*
When you move to another country, you have to <u>get used to</u> lots of different customs.
In California, I <u>used to sleep</u> outside in the summer because it was so warm.

1. .... is used to talk about something that happened regularly or was true in the past, but is different or not true now.
2. .... is used to talk about something which we are/were familiar with because we have done it often and it is not strange any more.
3. .... is used to talk about something which you become/became familiar with because we have done it often and it is not strange any more.

5 Complete these lists, then discuss them in small groups.

Living in my own country I'm used to:
1. ....
2. ....
3. ....

If I lived in Britain, I might find it difficult to get used to:
1. ....
2. ....
3. ....

6 ▭ We asked some people for things that foreign visitors to Britain might not be used to. Listen to their ideas and make notes. Compare your answers with a partner and your own answers to Exercise 5.

NATURE'S REMEDIES   vocabulary: health

1 Work with a partner and use a dictionary to check the meaning and pronunciation of any new words in the box.

> to suffer from   nausea / travel sickness   to be bitten by an insect (an insect bite)
> to be stung by a bee (a bee sting)   to feel itchy
> to have a cold / flu / bronchitis / cold sores / blocked sinuses / a sore throat / a wart

Tell your partner which of them you have experienced. Don't tell them any you don't want to talk about.

Example: *I sometimes suffer from travel sickness in the back of a car.*
I've never had warts.
I was bitten by mosquitoes last summer.

2 Label the items in the picture.

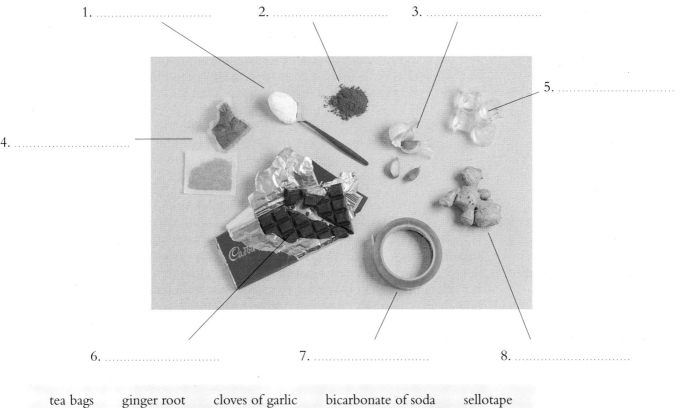

1. ....
2. ....
3. ....
5. ....
4. ....
6. ....
7. ....
8. ....

> tea bags   ginger root   cloves of garlic   bicarbonate of soda   sellotape
> cayenne pepper   ice cubes   a bar of chocolate

3 Some doctors believe that many natural substances are better than antibiotics for certain minor health problems. Can you guess which item on the left helps with the problems on the right? Work with a partner.

ginger root	fights colds and flu
sellotape	warms cold feet
cayenne pepper	relieves itching
ice	soothes cold sores
bicarbonate of soda	relieves nausea
garlic	gets rid of warts
a tea bag	relieves insect bites and blocked sinuses

4 ☐☐ ☐☐ Listen to the recording to check your answers. Then listen again, and make notes on any more information you learn about each remedy.

5 Discuss these questions in small groups.

1. Do you think these remedies could work?
2. Which ones would you be prepared to try?
3. What other remedies have you tried for the ailments in Exercise 3?
4. Did they work?

6 With a partner, write down some more remedies, using the verbs in Exercise 3. Make some of them true and some of them false.

Example: *Aspirin relieves toothache.*
         Wearing paper clips in your hair gets rid of flu.

Pass them to another pair. Can they work out which are true?

1 The front door of a building was changed from a simple door to a revolving one because of *feng shui*. A woman moved out of her apartment within a week because of *feng shui*. A man installed a tank with six black fish and hung a red clock in his office because of *feng shui*.

What do you think *feng shui* might be? Discuss with a partner.

2 📁 Listen to the recording about *feng shui*. Were your ideas correct? Listen again and answer the questions.

1. What is the general philosophy of *feng shui*?
2. What does a *feng shui* priest do?

3. Where is *feng shui* practised?
4. How were two people's lives affected by *feng shui*?

3 Discuss these points in small groups.

1. Is *feng shui* similar to any belief, science or superstition in your own culture? If so, in what ways?
2. What factors do *you* think about when you are placing your furniture in your home, room or workplace?

4 Check that you understand the abstract nouns in the box, then complete the second column, using a dictionary if necessary.

Noun	Adjective
success	successful
power	....
-----	-----
health	....
wealth	....
luck	....
-----	-----
philosophy	....
environment	....
-----	-----
wisdom	....
poverty	....

5 Read these sentences from the recording.

1. *If* you change your surroundings, you can change your life.
2. *Unless* she moved, she wouldn't survive.

We can say the second sentence like this:

If she didn't move, she wouldn't survive.   or   *If she stayed in her house, she wouldn't survive.*

What does *unless* mean?

6 Now complete these sentences in your own words, then compare and discuss your answers in small groups.

1. If you want to be successful, ...
2. Unless we do something about our environment, ...
3. Poverty will increase in developing countries unless ....
4. Good health is vital if ....
5. Unless you are very lucky, you can't ....
6. If people have too much power, ...

PERSONAL STUDY WORKBOOK

In your Personal Study Workbook, you will find more exercises to help you with your learning. For Unit 22, these include:

* exercises to practise *be/get used to* + *-ing*; and *if* and *unless*
* an activity to help you practise your pronunciation and read aloud fluently
* a recording about the problems people have adapting to things in other countries
* a story to write
* the last page of your visual dictionary to complete – animals and insects

---

REVIEW AND DEVELOPMENT

REVIEW OF UNIT 20

1 What's a work of art worth? | vocabulary: art and money |

Divide the list of words into the categories in the table.

Words to do with money and banking	Words to do with art and design	Words to do with both
....	....	....
....	....	....
....	....	....
....	....	....
....	....	....
....	....	....

an engraving	currency	forgery	to print	to issue a note
to decorate	a transaction	a merchant	coins	a portrait	a financier
a drawing	to be worth	a reproduction	an amount	to be in debt
a sculpture	to illustrate	landscape

Compare with a partner. Explain your decisions if necessary.

2 Drawings and engravings pronunciation: consonant clusters

A Look at the words in the list. Underline where two consonant sounds are next to each other.

Example: rep<u>l</u>ace   tran<u>sac</u><u>ti</u>on

How are the clusters pronounced? Say them with a partner, then listen to the recording to see if you were right.

studio   portrait   taxpayer   sculpture   merchant   suspicious
display   construction   engraving   drawing   landscape   reproduction

B Listen to these sentences and practise saying them.

1. It was an exhibition of drawings and engravings.
2. The sculptures were part of a large collection.
3. He buys a lot of reproduction furniture.
4. It was a very intricate portrait.
5. She is a magnificent landscape artist.
6. The statue was on display in the entrance to the gallery.

Now write two more sentences using the words above and read them to your partner.

3 An amazing article articles: *a, an, the* and zero article

Read this story, translated from a Swiss consumer magazine.
Then work with a partner and complete the text with *a/an* or *the* or nothing.

Can you eat curtains?

No, in general you can't. But read what happened to .... experienced housewife when she wanted to wash her curtains. They were delicate, so she washed them with care, but .... label on them did not give any clear instructions about how to wash them.

She decided to wash them in .... washing powder she always used, but .... curtains turned into .... kind of soft paste, something like cream cheese. She put .... paste into .... bowl to show her husband. Then she went out shopping.

Her husband returned before her, and feeling hungry, he cut .... slice of .... bread to eat with this sort of cream cheese on .... kitchen table.

'Even with plenty of salt and pepper, your cheese is quite tasteless,' he said to his wife when she came home. He went to bed but did not even suffer from .... indigestion.

REVIEW OF UNIT 21

1 In other words ... | vocabulary and paraphrasing |

Complete the sentences in a way that shows you understand the words underlined.

Example: *If you saw a film that was <u>dreadful</u>, it means* .you didn't like it or it was terrible.

1. If you find someone <u>amusing</u>, it means ....

....

2. Someone likes their coffee <u>weak</u>. In other words, ...

....

3. You were <u>thrilled</u> with the gift someone gave you. In other words, ...

....

4. If you are <u>satisfied</u> with the service in a restaurant, it means ....

....

5. A party you went to was <u>fun</u>. In other words, ...

....

6. If you are <u>exhausted</u> at the end of the day, it means ....

....

7. You find crossword puzzles <u>stimulating</u>. In other words, ...

....

8. If you applied for a job and were <u>unsuccessful</u>, it means ....

....

9. You found yesterday's lesson <u>challenging</u>. In other words, ...

....

Work in small groups and compare your sentence endings.

2 Complete the sentences | past conditional |

Divide into two groups. Group A must complete the sentences below in a logical way, while Group B does the same with the sentences on page 172. When you have finished, find someone from the other group and compare your sentences.

A 1. I would've told him the truth ....
   2. .... if I'd woken up earlier.
   3. If I had found the money, ...
   4. ...., I would've broken a window to get in.

GRAMMAR REFERENCE

PAST SIMPLE

Uses

1. To talk about past events and situations which are completed at a specific or known time:

   We saw them a week ago.
   She lived there for ten years. (She doesn't live there now.)

2. To talk about regular or repeated activities in the past, which don't happen now:

   When I was at school, we did homework every night.
   She never spoke to me at work.

Forms

Positive and negative

I		
You	came	
He	didn't (did not) come	
She	arrived	yesterday.
We	didn't arrive	
They		

Regular verbs end in *-d* (*arrived*) or *-ed* (*painted*) in the positive form.

Questions

Did	he	
Didn't	she	tell you?
	we	
	etc.	

WILL (FOR PREDICTION)

Use

To talk about the future, when we are saying what we think will happen (predictions):

I think there will be more cars on the roads in 20 years' time.
Most people won't write things by hand in the future.

Going to do is also used for prediction, especially when there is evidence now of the future situation:

Look at those clouds – it's going to rain.

Forms

I		
You		
He		
She	'll (will)	be late.
We	won't (will not)	
You		
They		

PRESENT CONTINUOUS

Uses

1. To talk about things happening now, at the moment of speaking:

   Be quiet! I'm working.
   I can see the children – they're playing in the garden.

2. To talk about something which is temporary and happening around now, but not necessarily at the moment of speaking:

   I'm doing a typing course. (I started last week and it finishes in two months.)
   They're showing Rambo again at the cinema. (It's on this week.)

3. To talk about a planned future arrangement:

   I'm having lunch with some friends.
   We're meeting them at the cinema at 7 o'clock.

This use of the present continuous is very similar to the *going to* future, and we could use *going to* in all cases. But if the plan includes an arrangement with others, most native speakers often prefer to use the present continuous. For plans that do not include arrangements with others, we use *going to*. Compare:

a. *I'm seeing my uncle this evening.* (It is arranged and my uncle knows about it.)
b. *I'm going to see my uncle this evening.* (It is my plan. My uncle may know about it, or he may not.)

Forms

Positive and negative

I	'm (am)	
	'm not	
He		
She	's (is)	
It	isn't (is not)	working.
We		
You	're (are)	
They	aren't (are not)	

Questions

	am	I	
		he	
	is	she	
What		it	doing?
		we	
	are	you	
		they	

2

COMPARATIVE AND SUPERLATIVE ADJECTIVES

Forms

ONE SYLLABLE ADJECTIVES
Add *-er* to make a comparative;
add *-est* to make a superlative:

old older the oldest
short shorter the shortest

Spelling notes:
1. one syllable adjectives ending in *-e*, add *-r* and *-st*:

wide wider widest

2. one syllable adjectives with consonant–vowel–consonant form double the last consonant:

fat fatter fattest
big bigger biggest

THREE OR MORE SYLLABLE ADJECTIVES
Add *more* before the adjective to make comparatives;
add *the most* before the adjective to make superlatives:

more expensive the most expensive
more reliable the most reliable

TWO SYLLABLE ADJECTIVES
Normally these follow the rules for three syllables:

more boring the most boring
more useful the most useful

except:
adjectives ending in *-y*, change to *i* and add *-er* or *-est*:

happy happier happiest

IRREGULAR ADJECTIVES

good better best
bad worse worst
little less least
much more most

Some words and expressions can also be used to modify comparatives:

*It's **a bit** colder today.* (a small difference)
*The weather was **much** better last week.*
*It's a **far** more interesting book than her last one.* (a big difference)

Other words and expressions that can be used in this way are *a great deal, very much, a lot, a little,* and *no.*

UNCOUNTABLE NOUNS

Uncountable nouns only have one form. They do not have a plural form; they cannot be used with a plural verb; they are not normally used with the indefinite article *a* or *an*:

*I asked them for **some information**.*
*Their **advice was** very useful.*
*I've got **too much equipment** here.*

There are some uncountable nouns in English which are countable in other languages. These cause particular problems, and common examples include:

information advice travel luggage baggage money
homework knowledge furniture traffic research
spaghetti progress news machinery equipment

COUNTABLE AND UNCOUNTABLE

Some nouns may be countable (C) with one meaning but uncountable (U) with another:

*He's got long black **hair**.* (U)
*There's a **hair** (C) on your dinner plate.*
*She has 20 years' **experience** (U) in banking.*
*My holiday in India was a fantastic **experience**.* (C)
*I love **coffee**.* (U)
*Would you like a **coffee**?* (C) (= a cup of coffee)

3

-ING FORM OR INFINITIVE

When certain verbs are immediately followed by another verb, the second verb is an *-ing* form. For other verbs, the second verb is an infinitive.

Verbs followed by an *-ing* form

Some of these are verbs which mean *like* or *hate*. Here are the most common:

enjoy	*can't stand*	*detest* (= hate)
don't mind	*loathe* (= hate)	
dislike	*resent*	

GRAMMAR REFERENCE 159

Other common verbs followed by *-ing* form:

*admit avoid consider delay deny finish give up
imagine involve miss practise regret*

Verbs followed by an infinitive

Here are some of the most common examples:

*agree arrange attempt decide expect forget hope
offer promise refuse want would like*

Some verbs can be followed by an *-ing* form or infinitive. Often there will be a difference in meaning, but with these four examples, the difference is very small:

*love
like   to go …
hate   going …
intend*

PREPOSITION + *-ING* FORM

When a preposition is followed immediately by a verb, the verb is an *-ing* form:

*I'm worried **about** leaving them on their own.
I'm not interested **in** listening to music.
She insisted **on** paying for the meal.*

4

PRESENT PERFECT

Uses

1. a. To talk about events and situations in one's life, up to the present time. We don't know when these things happened:

   ***I've** never **worked** in a bank.
   Have you ever **been** to Athens?
   My brother **has written** articles for a magazine.* (in his life)

   Ever and *never* are common with this use.

   Compare:
   *My brother **has worked** for a magazine.*
   (It is an experience in his life so far.)
   and
   *My brother **worked** for a magazine a few years ago.*
   (We know when, so we use the past simple.)

   b. To talk about an action or situation in a limited and unfinished period of time:

   ***Have you read** any magazines **this week**?* (This week is not yet finished.)
   ***Have you written** your article **yet**?
   I **haven't seen** the editor **yet**.*
   (Yet is used in questions and negatives, and refers to something up to the present time.)

2. To talk about an action or a situation which started in the past and which continues up to the present:

   *Since I joined the company, **I've been** to six different countries.* (I am still with the company.)
   ***I've worked** here for two years.* (I still work here.)
   *How long **have you had** that car?* (I still have it.)

   Compare:
   ***I've worked** here for two years.* (I still do.)
   ***I worked** here for two years.* (I worked here some time ago – now I don't.)

   For, since and *how long …?* are common with this use. *For* is used with periods of time:

   for two years, for a week

   Since is used with a point in time:

   since last May, since 1992, since I started work here

Forms

Positive and negative

		Past Participle	
I You	've (not) have(n't)	heard	
He She	's (not) has(n't)	done	it.
We They	've (not) have(n't)	eaten	

Questions

Have	you		
Has	he she	done	it?
Have	we they		

5

POSSESSIVE *'S*

Use

We use *'s* and not a preposition construction to talk about possession. We normally add *'s* to singular nouns and *s'* to plural nouns. Irregular plural nouns have *'s*.

*John's mother (John is singular.)
the boy's teachers (There is only one boy.)
the boys' teachers (There are a number of boys.)
the children's toys (Children is an irregular plural.)*

PROBABILITY AND POSSIBILITY

Use

There are a number of ways of expressing possibility and probability in English:

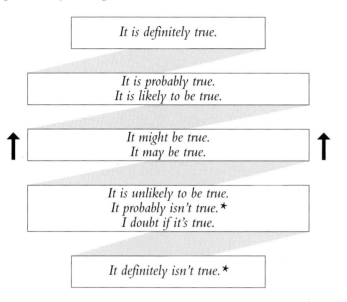

It is definitely true.

It is probably true. It is likely to be true.

It might be true. It may be true.

It is unlikely to be true. It probably isn't true.★ I doubt if it's true.

It definitely isn't true.★

★ Notice that the position of the adverbs *probably* and *definitely* changes in the negative forms

PREPOSITIONS IN *WH-* QUESTIONS

In *wh-* questions, (*when, who, what*, etc.) it is common with verbs which need a preposition to find the preposition at the end, particularly in informal English:

> *Who could you talk **to**?*
> *What did you ask her **about**?*

If you put the preposition at the beginning, you need to change *who* to *whom*, and the question becomes extremely formal in style. This form is rare in spoken English:

> *To whom did you speak?*

6

PAST CONTINUOUS

Uses

1. We can use it to contrast a situation over a period of time (what was happening) with an event or action of a shorter duration (what happened):

> *He was washing his hair when he heard a noise.*

> *He was washing his hair* was the situation, or the background to the noise, which was a simple action.

> *I sat down and ordered a drink. Three men were playing cards in a corner of the bar.*

> The three men started playing before I sat down, and continued after I sat down.

2. We also use the past continuous to describe a scene in a story:

> *The sun was just setting.*
> *People were going home from work.*

Form

was/were + present participle

Positive and negative

I You She/He	was(n't) were(n't) was(n't)	working.
It	was(n't)	raining.
We They	were(n't) were(n't)	going out.

Questions

Was it raining? Were they waiting?

WHILE AND *WHEN*

When can mean *during that time* or *at that time*.

> *I met her when I was living in Madrid.*
> (*when* = during the time when I was living in Madrid)
> *We were very pleased when the parcel arrived.*
> (*when* = at that time)

While means during that time:

> *I met her while I was living in Madrid.*

You cannot use *while* to mean *at that time*.
While is often (but not always) followed by the past continuous.

PHRASAL VERBS

A phrasal verb is a verb + adverbial particle, and often the meaning is different from the meaning of the two separate parts, e.g. *give up something* = *stop doing something*.
Some phrasal verbs are intransitive and are not followed by an object:

> *Please **sit down**.*
> *Why did the car **break down**?*
> *I always **get up** at eight o'clock.*

Other phrasal verbs are transitive (followed by a direct object). The two parts of a transitive phrasal verb can usually be separated, and if the object is a noun, it can go before or after the particle:

> *He's turning **the light** on.*
> *He's turning on **the light**.*

If the object is a pronoun, it must go between the verb and the particle:

> *He's turning **it** on.*
> not *He's turning on **it**.*

GET + PAST PARTICIPLE AND REFLEXIVE PRONOUNS

Uses

1. When *get* is followed by a *past participle*, the meaning may be similar to a passive form, with *get* as the auxiliary:

   I got bitten. (= something bit me)
   I got attacked. (= somebody/something attacked me)

   We often use this construction to talk about something that happens very suddenly or unexpectedly (we don't expect to get bitten or attacked).

2. We can also use *get* with a limited number of past participles to talk about things we do to ourselves:

   *I **got dressed**, went out and **got lost**.*
   *She's **getting married** next week.* (The verb *to marry* is possible but far less common.)

   Other languages often use reflexive pronouns to talk about things we do to ourselves. In English, we don't use reflexive pronouns for things we normally do to ourselves:

   *I **got dressed**.* (Not *I dressed myself*, unless we want to emphasise the fact: for instance, if you had been ill, but managed to dress yourself without help.)
   *I **had a wash**.* (Not *I washed myself*, unless we want to emphasise the fact.)

   In other situations, when the subject and object of a verb are the same, we do use reflexive pronouns:

   *She **cut herself** on the glass.*
   *Mark **hurt himself** playing tennis.*

Form

I		myself.	We		ourselves.
You		yourself.	You	cut	yourselves.
He	cut	himself.	They		themselves.
She		herself.			
It		itself.			

7

UNCOUNTABLE NOUNS ENDING IN *-S*

Some nouns which end in *-s* look as if they are plural but, in fact, they are singular, so they require a singular verb:

   Maths *is my favourite subject.*
   Economics *is easy for some people.*

Most nouns of this type refer to subjects and activities and Unit 7 includes almost all the common examples.

DEFINING RELATIVE CLAUSES (1)

1. Look at these examples:

   *I gave it to the man **who** (or **that**) lives over there.*
   *The thing **which** (or **that**) changed my life was university.*

   In these sentences *who* and *which* are the subjects (*the man* and *the thing*) of the verbs (*lives* and *changed*), so they must stay in the sentence.

2. Now look at these examples:

   *This is the man (**who**/**that**) we saw.*
   *Where are the books (**which**/**that**) we ordered?*

   Here *who*, *that* and *which* are the objects (*the man* and *the books*) of the verbs (*saw* and *ordered*), and we can leave them out. This is particularly common in spoken English. In very formal English we can also use *whom* instead of *who* when it is the object of the verb in the relative clause, but in spoken English it isn't common.

For the main information on relative clauses, see Grammar Reference 13.

ADJECTIVE + INFINITIVE

Many adjectives can be followed by the infinitive:

   *I found it **difficult** to understand her.*
   *It's **impossible** to get there by 9 o'clock.*

Other common adjectives that can be used in this way are:

easy   possible   happy   surprised   important   boring   nice   interesting   afraid   pleased

Too and *enough* are often used with this construction:

   *I am **too** old to play football.*
   *It's not warm **enough** to take my coat off.*

VERB + OBJECT + INFINITIVE

Ask and *tell* are two of the most common verbs which can be used in this way:

   She asked us to leave.
   I told them to wait.

Other common verbs that can be used in this way are *want, advise, persuade, encourage, beg.*

OBLIGATION

See Grammar Reference 9 for Obligation.

8

LINK WORDS: CONCESSION/CONTRAST, ADDITION, RESULT

Concession/Contrast

When we accept one fact, argument or opinion, but we then want to put another fact, argument or opinion against it (often in contrast), we signal it with particular link words or phrases:

*The food was good quality **but** it was very expensive.*
***Although** she worked very hard, she failed her exams.*
*(She failed her exams, **although** she worked very hard.)*
***In spite of** the weather, they still went for a walk.*
(In spite of the fact that it was raining, they still went for a walk.)
*It looks as if it's going to be a nice day. **On the other hand**, it could easily cloud over and rain for the rest of the afternoon.*
*He found the course very stressful. **However**, he still enjoyed it.*

Note:

In the first three examples, the two elements are combined in one sentence. In the last two examples, the linkers often (but not always) connect ideas from two sentences.

Addition

When we want to emphasise a piece of information or argument, or we want to add an extra piece of information or argument, we can use a number of link words and phrases:

*They broke the window and damaged the table. They **also** got dirt all over the carpet.*
*Her new job sounds more interesting than the old one; it has a better salary **as well**. (We could also use too here.)*
*The new offices will give us much more space. **In addition**, they all have air conditioning, so they will be more comfortable. (We could use moreover or furthermore here.)*

Moreover and *furthermore* are used in more formal contexts in English.

Result

*We ordered the taxi for 4 o'clock, but it didn't come until 4.40. **As a result**, we were late. (We could also use so or consequently here.)*

OBLIGATION

We can use different structures to express an obligation:

*We **have to***
*You **are obliged to*** *work at weekends.*

In the present or future we can also use *must*, but the above structures are used for obligation in the past:

*We **had to** wear a uniform at school.*
*We **were obliged to** stay until the end of the film.*

Be obliged to is used in more formal contexts in English.

'Moral' obligation

We sometimes use *be supposed to* and *be expected to* when we talk about a rule, custom or duty; and they often have the force of a 'moral obligation':

*You**'re supposed to** take your shoes off in a Japanese house.* (That is the custom/rule)
*Branch managers **are expected to** work at weekends if necessary.* (It is considered a duty)

Sometimes when they are used to express a rule or law, there may be a suggestion that some people do not observe it. Compare:

*You **have to** wear a seat belt in a car.* (The speaker is saying this is the law – there is no choice.)
*You**'re supposed to** wear a seat belt in a car.* (The speaker may be suggesting this is a law that some people do not obey.)

No obligation

When something is not necessary we can express it in different ways:

*You **don't have to** work on Saturday.* (= You can if you want, but it isn't necessary.)
*You**'re not obliged to** do homework.*
*When I lived there I **didn't have to** pay any rent.*

Don't confuse *don't have to* with *mustn't* (see below).

PROHIBITION

This means something is forbidden, not permitted:

*You **can't** stay here after six o'clock.*
*You**'re not allowed to** smoke in here.*
*We **couldn't** wear make-up at school.*
*When I was 12 I **wasn't allowed to** go out after nine o'clock.*

We can also express prohibition in the present or future using *mustn't*, but this is more commonly used to express something that is wrong or dangerous:

*You **mustn't** swim near those rocks.* (It's dangerous.)
*You **mustn't** hit children.* (It's wrong.)

PERMISSION

Basically the opposite of prohibition, thus:

*You **can** stay here as long as you like.*
*You**'re allowed to** use a dictionary in the exam.*

Note:

We do not normally say something *is/isn't allowed*; we say *you're allowed to* or *you aren't allowed to/you're not allowed to*:

A: *Can we use the car park at the back?*
B: *No, you**'re not allowed to**.*

THE PASSIVE

Use

We sometimes use the passive when we are more interested in the person or thing *affected by an action*, and not the person or thing *responsible for the action*:

*The books **are ordered** every month.* (We are more interested in the books than who orders them.)
*The man **was arrested** outside his home.* (We are interested in the man, and not the person who arrested him.)
*Children should **be protected**.* (We are more interested in the children than who protects them.)

The passive is also quite common in notices when we want to sound more formal or impersonal:

*Shoplifters **will be prosecuted**.*
*Passengers **are requested** to keep their seat belts fastened.*

From these examples you can see that the person or thing responsible for the action is often not given. This is because in these cases, we are probably not interested in them, and sometimes we don't know who or what they are.

However, it is possible to mention the *agent* or doer at the end of the clause, and if you do, it will give more emphasis to the agent:

*All these paintings were done **by prisoners**.*
*The children were looked after **by teenagers staying in the hotel**.*

Forms

The passive is formed by the verb *to be* + the past participle of the verb. The only tense change is to the verb *to be*:

I	am/was/will be	+ past participle (e.g. ordered, taken)
He She It	is/was/will be	+ past participle (e.g. found, injured)
You We They	are/were/will be	+ past participle (e.g. asked, given)

USED TO (DO)

To talk about something which happened regularly in the past, or was true for some time in the past, but is different or not true now:

*She **used to** work in a factory when she was young.*
*There **used to be** a factory where the library is now.*
*He **used to** visit his aunt every week.*

Forms

Positive and negative

I You He/She We They	used to didn't use to	work in a factory.

In spoken English, *never used to* is often preferred to *didn't use to*:

*They **never used to** stay longer than half an hour.*

Questions

Did	you he she they	use to	work here?

WOULD

To talk about something which happened regularly in the past:

*He **would** visit his aunt every week.*
*When they were younger they **would** watch TV for hours.*

However, it can only be used for repeated actions. It cannot be used to talk about states and situations:

          used to
She ~~would~~ work in a factory when she was young.
          used to
He ~~would~~ have a beard, but he shaved it off because his wife didn't like it.

11

IF SENTENCES WITH *WILL, MAY, MIGHT*

Use

To talk about situations which are possible or likely to happen:

If you buy a camera, the salesperson
    will   (sure)
    might   *try to sell you a film.* (perhaps)
    may   (perhaps)

Forms

If + present simple, *will*
won't (will not)
may
might
+ verb

TO HAVE SOMETHING DONE

Use

To talk about services which people do for you and which you often pay for:

We had the house painted last summer.
Have you had your hair cut?
I'd like to have these trousers cleaned, please.

Compare:

We had the house painted last summer.
(Someone else did it and we paid for it.)
We painted the house last summer.
(We did it ourselves.)

Form

to have something done
have + object + past participle

12

ADVERBS: *VERY* AND *ABSOLUTELY*

When we want to intensify or emphasise certain adjectives, we can use *very* and *absolutely* before the adjective. We use *very* before *gradable* adjectives, and *absolutely* before adjectives which express *an extreme quality*:

very	*big*	*absolutely*	*enormous*
	good		*fantastic*
	small		*tiny*

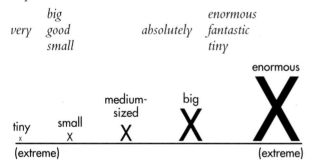

In spoken English we also use *really* a lot, and we use it before both types of adjective:

really big and *really enormous*; *really good* and *really fantastic*.

13

IF SENTENCES WITH *WOULD* AND *MIGHT* (SECOND CONDITIONAL)

Use

To talk about improbable or imaginary situations in the present or future:

If I won the race, I would be very happy.
(The speaker doesn't think that he/she will win the race.)
If I had a house in the mountains, I would go there every week.
(The speaker hasn't got a house in the mountains.)
He might get married if he met the right person.
(He hasn't met the right person up to now, but if he did, it is *possible* that he would get married.)

Forms

If + past simple, and *would* or *might* + infinitive without *to* in the main clause.

IF PAST SIMPLE,	WOULD/MIGHT + VERB
If they invited us,	we might go.
I were rich,	I would give my money to you.
	I'd give …
we didn't have a car,	we wouldn't go out so much.

Note:

1. We use the past simple tense in the *if* clause, but we are *not* talking about past time.
2. With the verb *to be*, we use *were* for all persons (If I/you/he/she/we/they were …).
   In conversation, people sometimes say *If I was rich* or *If he was rich*. (This form is not used in formal English.)

DEFINING RELATIVE CLAUSES (2)

Look at these examples:

*I haven't met the man **who gave him the money**.*
*Where's the film **which I bought last week**?*
*The place **where they work** is beautiful.*

The underlined parts of these sentences are relative clauses, and each one identifies or defines the noun it is used with: in the first sentence it defines *the man*; in the second it defines *the film*; and in the third it defines *the place*.

When we are defining people we use *who*, and when we are defining things we use *which*; in many situations we can also use *that* in place of *who* or *which*:

*I haven't met the man **that** gave him the money.*
*Where's the film **that** I bought last week?*

In spoken English, *that* is often preferred to *which*, and sometimes preferred to *who*.

When we are defining places we use *where*.

For more information on relative clauses see Grammar Reference 7.

LINK WORDS: SIMILARITIES AND DIFFERENCES

We can express similarities and differences between different subjects with these structures:

*Paul is **similar to** Tom **in that** they both love football.*
*Mike is **different from** Paul and Tom **in that** he hates football.*

If this difference is the only one – in other words the exception – we can express it in this way:

*Mike is similar to the other boys **except that** he hates football.*

When we just want to express a very clear contrast, often between two subjects, we can use *while* or *whereas*:

*Saturday is very busy **whereas** Sunday is fairly quiet.*
*Paul spends all day playing football **while** Mike is only interested in his computer.*

Note:

For more information about different link words see Grammar Reference 8.

14

PAST PERFECT SIMPLE

Use

When we are talking about the past, we use the past perfect to refer to an earlier event, i.e. before the period or moment we are talking about:

*We arrived at seven o'clock. The others **had been** there for half an hour.* (= half an hour before we arrived)

```
                              NOW
    X               X          X
  the others ...... 30 ...... we
   arrived        mins      arrived
```

*I **saw** a lovely dress in the window but unfortunately I **had spent** all my money.* (= before I saw the dress)

For this reason, the past perfect is often used with time conjunctions:

***When** I got there the train **had left**.*
*I went home **after I'd spoken** to her.*

Note:

1. With *after* and *before*, the time sequence is often very clear and the past perfect is not necessary. In the above sentence it is possible to say *I went home after I spoke to her*.
2. If we talk about past events in the order they happened, we also do not need the past perfect:

   *We **sat down**, **had** a coffee, then we **went** for a walk and **took** a taxi home.*

   If we change the order of events, we may decide to use the past perfect:

   *We **sat down** and **had** a coffee, and then we **took** a taxi home after we **had been** for a walk.*

Form

Positive and negative

Had/Hadn't (had not)		+ Past participle
I		
You		worked.
He/She/It	had(n't)	gone.
We		seen.
They		

Questions

Had	you he/she/it they	left by then?

15

PRESENT PERFECT CONTINUOUS (vs. SIMPLE)

Uses

1. When we talk about an activity or situation that began in the past and has continued up to the present moment, we can often use the present perfect simple or continuous with very little difference in meaning:

   I've lived here since 1993.
   I've been living here since 1993.

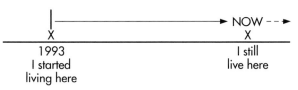

```
   |─────────────────────────► NOW - - ►
   X                            X
  1993                       I still
  I started                 live here
  living here
```

Note:

As with other continuous verb forms though, we don't normally use the present perfect continuous with state verbs such as *know*, *understand* or *seem*:

I've known him for ten years.
(not *I've been knowing him for ten years.*)

2. The present perfect simple is used for an activity that happened in a period before now (the time is not given). If we use the present perfect continuous, it suggests that the activity is not complete:

   He has done the housework. (And has finished it.)
   He has been doing the housework. (Perhaps he has stopped the activity for the moment, but he hasn't finished.)

---

3. We often use the present perfect continuous when we want to emphasise the result or effect of an activity (after the activity has finished):

You've been doing the housework. (The house is very clean.)
It's been raining. (The roads are wet.)
She's been cooking. (What a wonderful smell.)

Form

The present perfect continuous is formed with *have been* or *has been* followed by an *-ing* form:

Positive and negative

I You We They	have been haven't been (have not been)	living. working. waiting.
He She It	has been hasn't been (has not been)	living. waiting.

Questions

Have you been working? Have they been running? Has she been waiting? Has it been raining?

16

WISH + PAST SIMPLE

Use

To talk about a situation in the present that we would like to be different:

I wish I had a good dictionary. (I haven't got one.)
I wish I could swim. (I can't swim.)
I wish I didn't have to go out this evening. (I have to.)

Forms

wish + past simple form

Note:

1. The past simple tense here does *not* carry the meaning of past time; it is similar to the use of the past simple in *if* sentences.

2. With the verb *to be*, you can use *was* or *were*:

I wish I $\begin{matrix} was \\ were \end{matrix}$ *somewhere else.*

Was is more informal and mostly used in speech.

NEGATION

Negative forms of verbs

a. Simple tenses (present simple, past simple): add ***not (n't)*** to the auxiliary *do, does, did*.

I	don't (do not)	
He	doesn't (does not)	go out late.
They	didn't (did not)	

b. Auxiliary verbs (*be, have, can, must,* etc.): add ***not (n't)*** to the auxiliary:

It isn't raining.   *It's not raining.*
I can't come tonight.   *We haven't got time.*

c. *Every, some, any, no*

every	some	any	no/none
everyone/ everybody	someone/ somebody	anyone/ anybody	no-one/ nobody
everything	something	anything	nothing
everywhere	somewhere	anywhere	nowhere

Note:
*She has **no** friends.* (positive verb)
*She doesn**'t** have **any** friends.* (negative verb)

but **not** *She doesn't have no friends.*

d. Other notes
   • Negative forms of:

   I hope so.   I hope not.
   I'm afraid so.   I'm afraid not.
   but
   I think so.   I don't think so.

   • The verb *think* usually attracts the negative idea in a sentence:

   I don't think they'll come.
   rather than
   I think they won't come.

   • *So* and *neither*
   We use *so* + auxiliary + subject (*So do I, So have we,* etc.) to agree with a positive statement:

   A: *I like Mozart.*
   B: *So do I.*

   We use *neither* + auxiliary + subject (*Neither do I, Neither have we,* etc.) to agree with a negative statement:

   A: *I haven't got any money.*
   B: *Neither have I.*

17

PARTITIVES

When you want to talk about the quantity of something, you can use a word describing the quantity + *of* + the noun:

A bit of paper
A group of people
A drop of milk

We often use this structure to describe a container and its contents:

A carton of milk
A tube of toothpaste
A jug of water

With some of these containers it is quite common to add *-ful*. Here are the most common examples:

A bucketful of water
A cupful of washing-up powder
A spoonful of salt

We can even add *-ful* to some nouns to create quantities:

A handful of rice
A mouthful of water

REPORTED SPEECH

When we reproduce someone's words or thoughts, we can do it through their exact words:

He came in and said 'I'm going to marry her'.
'I won't help him,' she said.

Or we can use reported speech, which means we often make certain changes:

1. We use a reporting verb – *say* and *tell* are the most common.
2. Pronouns may change (see table below for examples).
3. In formal written English, and sometimes in spoken English, the tense moves back:

DIRECT SPEECH	REPORTED SPEECH
'I like it.'	She said she liked it.
'I'm leaving.'	He told me he was leaving.
'She took it.'	He said she had taken it.
'They've gone.'	She told me they had gone.
'He had already left.'	They said he had already left. (no change)
'I'll tell him.'	He said he would tell him.

Would, could, should, ought and *might* do not change from direct speech to reported speech.

In less formal written English, and sometimes in spoken English, we don't make these changes. These variations are all possible:

*He **says he's** going to marry her.*
*He **said he's** going to marry her.*
*He **said** he **was** going to marry her.*

One reason for not changing tense is when we are reporting a fact which is still true:

'London is bigger than Paris.'
He said London is bigger than Paris. (It was then, and still is.)

In spoken English, you also find the use of the past continuous (instead of the past simple) in the reporting verb:

*He **was telling** me (that) he's very busy.*
*She **was saying** (that) they had lost all their money.*

Other changes in reported speech are to certain words. For example:

*'I saw him **yesterday**.'*
*He said he he'd seen him **the day before**.*
*'I bought it **here**.'*
*He said he'd bought it **there**.*

REPORTED QUESTIONS

There are some important points to remember when reporting questions in English:

- You do not treat them as questions by using interrogative word order: you use affirmative word order.
- You do not put a question mark at the end.
- You do not use the auxiliary *do/does/did* that you use in direct questions.
- There are two main types of question and two types of report structure.

Report structures for questions

1. Yes/no questions

   When you report a yes/no question, you use an *if clause* (and sometimes a *whether clause*):

   Do you speak German?
   *He asked her **if she spoke German**.*
   Did you see them last night?
   *He asked her **if she had seen them last night**.*

   Notice that the tense still moves back one, as in reported speech.

2. *Wh-* questions

   You still use the *wh-* word in the reported question, but the word order is different and there is no auxiliary *do/did*.

   How often do you go there?
   *He asked her **how often she went there**.*
   Where have they gone?
   *He asked her **where they had gone**.*
   Why did you phone?
   *He asked her **why she had phoned**.*

SHOULD, OUGHT (TO), AND HAD BETTER

Use

Should, ought (to) and *had better* have a similar meaning if you want to give advice or an opinion about a specific problem:

	should	
You	*ought to*	*go and see the doctor if you don't feel well.*
	'd better	

	shouldn't	
We	*ought not to*	*park the car in front of the gates.*
	'd better not	

(*Ought not to* is often avoided in spoken English.)

We don't use *had better* with general advice, however:

	should	
A grammar book	*ought to*	*explain things clearly.*

not
A grammar book had better explain things clearly.

Form

The form remains the same for all persons:

Should + infinitive without *to*
Should not (*shouldn't*) + infinitive without *to*
Should we + infinitive without *to* …?
Ought to

VERB + *-ING* (OR INFINITIVE)

See Grammar Reference 3 for the main information about this point of grammar.

Try is an unusual verb because it can be followed by an *-ing* form or an infinitive, but the meaning is different. Followed by an *-ing* form the meaning of *try* is *experiment*; followed by an infinitive, it means *to attempt something that is often difficult.* Compare:

*If the book is not on my desk, **try** look**ing** in the cupboard.*
*He's very busy but you could **try** phon**ing** him.*
with:
*I **tried to get** a job in Sweden for about six months.*
*The government is **trying to reach** an agreement.*

Another verb which operates in a similar way is *remember.* Compare:

*I **remember** see**ing** that film.* (= it is in my memory)
*Do you **remember** tak**ing** off your necklace?* (= is it in your memory?)
with:
*I **remembered to post** the letter.* (= I didn't forget.)
***Remember to wake** me before seven.* (= don't forget)

PREPOSITION + *-ING*

See Grammar Reference 3 for information about this point of grammar.

ADJECTIVE + INFINITIVE

See Grammar Reference 7 for information about this point of grammar.

ARTICLES

Definite article or indefinite article?

We use the definite article *the* before a noun when the listener and speaker know which thing or person they are talking about, or if there is only one example of the thing. When we don't know which one, or it's one of many, or it isn't important to know, we use the indefinite article *a/an* (sometimes we may also use *some* or no article):

*I saw **a** girl in **the** chemist's this morning.*
(The speaker and listener know *which* chemist's [perhaps there is only one], but so far, the speaker has not defined *which* girl.)
*You can buy **a** copy of **the** watch in his painting.*
(It is *a* copy because it is one of many copies; but *the* watch because there is only one in his painting.)

Definite article or zero article?

We don't use any article with plural nouns and uncountable nouns when we are talking about things in general. Compare:

*I like **dogs**.* (in general)
*I don't like **the dog next door**.* (a specific dog)
***Furniture** is expensive.* (in general)
***The furniture in their flat** is very old.* (specific furniture)

Note:
This is an important rule to learn because it is often different in other languages.

Definite article or zero article: special uses

We normally use *the* before:

rivers	oceans	seas	mountain ranges	groups of states
groups of islands	cinemas	theatres	museums	hotels

We normally don't use *the* before:

lakes	mountains	people's names	streets	parks
continents	most countries			

Form

Articles include the definite article (*the*) and the indefinite article (*a/an*).

The indefinite article is *a/an* followed by singular countable nouns.
We use *an* before nouns which begin with the vowels *a, e, i, o*; with nouns which begin with the vowel *u* when it is pronounced /ʌ/ e.g. *an uncle, an umbrella* (but not when it is pronounced /juː/ e.g. *a uniform, a university*); and before nouns which begin with a silent *h*, e.g. *an hour*.
With all other nouns the indefinite article is *a*.

PASSIVES

See Grammar Reference 9 for information about passives.

LINK WORDS

See Grammar Reference 8 for information about link words of concession/contrast, addition, and result.

SHOULD HAVE + PAST PARTICIPLE

We use this construction to talk about an action in the past when you or someone else did something wrong and you are saying how it could have been avoided:

> *You should have saved the money.* (But you didn't.)
> *They should've sold the car.* (But they didn't.)
> *She should've phoned the police.* (But she didn't.)

PAST CONDITIONAL

Use

This form is used when people are imagining *the opposite of* or *something different from* what actually happened in the past, and they are describing the consequences:

> *If I **had known**, I **would have told** him.* (= but I didn't know, so I couldn't tell him)
> *If she **had spoken** to them, they **wouldn't have sent** the letter.* (= she didn't see them, so they sent the letter)

We can also use *could* (= would be able) and *might* (= would perhaps) in these sentences:

> *If I **had had** more money, I **could have bought** that computer.*
> *He **might have helped** if you **had apologised** to him.*

Form

The past conditional is formed using *if* + past perfect, with the conditional perfect.

If	I had / I'd	known,	I would have / I would've	told him.

| If | she hadn't gone, | she wouldn't have missed them. |

| We | wouldn't've met | if I'd stayed at home. |

Contractions are common in both parts of the sentence in spoken English.

22

BE/GET USED TO + -ING

We use *be used to + -ing* to talk about something which we are (or were) familiar with because we have done it often and it is not strange any more (or we did it often in the past and it wasn't strange to us then):

> *I'm used to working at weekends.* (= I probably do it quite a lot; it's normal for me.)
> *When I lived on the farm I was used to getting up at 6 am.* (= It was normal for me at that time.)

We use *get used to + -ing* to talk about the process in which you become familiar with something, and it is not strange any more.

> *I'm getting used to drinking coffee in the morning.* (= It was strange, but now it's becoming more familiar.)

Note:

These structures should not be confused with *used to + infinitive* to talk about something that happened regularly or was true in the past, but is different or not true now:

> *I used to have a beard.* (= I don't have one now.)

See Grammar Reference 10 for more information about *used to + infinitive*.

ADDITIONAL MATERIAL

Unit 5 POSSIBLE INFLUENCES Exercise 4

First past the post

There are many theories about birth order and a great deal of research has been done. These are just some of the observations that many psychologists agree on:

● Parents talk to first-born babies *more* than to later children.

● Parents are less strict with later children than with their first child.

● First-born children use physical power to get what they want, whereas later children make more use of persuasion.

● *First-born* children are more bossy than *later* children.

● Later children also tell tales to their parents and teachers about other children.

● First-born children identify more strongly with their parents and are more influenced by them.

● *First-born* children have more communication with their parents than *later children*.

● First-born children are under more pressure to do well at school.

● Psychologists have a clearer idea of the personality of first-born children than of other children.

Unit 5 REVIEW AND DEVELOPMENT REVIEW OF UNIT 4: Exercise 1

9. I can't remember who I .... for in the last election.
10. The magazine is .... at women in their early twenties.
11. I just couldn't .... with all the problems at once.
12. They have .... a lot of money in that company.
13. We are .... of going to Canada for our holiday.
14. She .... from arthritis so she's in a lot of pain.
15. The man was .... for the murder of the young policewoman.
16. If you .... this film with her last film, you can see a big difference.

Unit 6 TURNING ON AND TURNING OFF Exercise 1

fasten	turn on	wrap up	pack
do up	plug in	load (up)	
get on	get into	lock	light
tie (up)			

Unit 11 CAN YOU SELL IT? Exercise 6

Amazing new Scientific

GUARANTEED to keep at least some of the rain off while you're cycling!!!

CYCLE UMBRELLA

ONLY £2.98 ON THE ROAD!

14 day delivery. Sorry no C.O.D.s
DEPT. 882.

Unit 11 REVIEW AND DEVELOPMENT REVIEW OF UNIT 10: Exercise 2

1. You telephone Mr Cartwright's secretary and ask to speak to Mr Cartwright. You work in the accounts department, and you need to speak to him urgently.
2. You receive a call from an old friend whom you haven't seen for several months. The last time you saw this friend, he/she lent you quite a lot of money and you haven't paid them back.
3. You're staying at your friend Josephine's house. She has gone on holiday with an old boyfriend for a week, but she doesn't want anyone to know.

Unit 13 THE JURY SYSTEM ON TRIAL Exercise 3

The other side of the coin

The jury system represents a person's fundamental right to be judged by his or her equals, that's to say, twelve men and women who come from different sections of society. It may not be a perfect system but what is the alternative? Judges come from a very narrow cross-section of society, so it would be impossible for them to represent the views of most ordinary people. And can we trust the opinion of one judge, or even two or three judges? With twelve ordinary people you should get a reasonably balanced judgement. And it also gives ordinary citizens responsibility in their community and a real sense of contributing to society. The jury system is expensive, and the cost is going up all the time, but do we want to live in a society where justice is decided by money? When we are making decisions about people's lives, we must do everything possible to be fair and just. Money should not be an issue in the discussion. A final point about the jury system is that most people believe it is the best and the fairest system. And it is very important that people have faith in their system of justice.

Unit 15 NEIGHBOURS Exercise 4

A neighbour's car alarm is driving Londoner Norman McKenzie crazy. The alarm is very sensitive to noise, vibration and even changes in the weather, and it has been going off as much as ten times every night for the last seven months.

'The police told me they couldn't do anything, and I was at my wit's end,' said Norman. So last week he took a metal pole and smashed the car windscreen. It's been repaired at McKenzie's expense, but unfortunately the alarm still keeps going off.

Unit 22 REVIEW AND DEVELOPMENT REVIEW OF UNIT 21: Exercise 2

B 1. .... if he'd asked me.
2. I wouldn't have been late ....
3. .... I would have taken it to the police.
4. If I'd forgotten my key, ...

ADDITIONAL MATERIAL

Unit 17 PACKAGE HOLIDAYS Exercise 5

TRAVEL AGENT HOLIDAY INFORMATION

TRANSFERS

For Lisbon the best option is to take a taxi from the airport to the city centre. It takes 20–30 minutes and costs less than £10.

INSURANCE

You are required to have travel insurance before you travel on one of the tours. We can arrange this (see below for details) or you can organise your own and provide details of the cover when you book.

Insurance Premiums
- Up to 3 nights   £11
- 4–5 nights   £14
- 6–7 nights   £17

IF YOU CHANGE YOUR BOOKING

If you want to change any details of your booking, e.g. departure date or airport, we will do our best to help. There will be a charge of £13 for this service.

EXCURSIONS

These are not included in the price of the holiday. The following excursions can be booked on arrival in Lisbon:

City tour   £19
Daily (half-day)

Sintra/Cabo da Roca/Estoril   £48
A day out to visit beautiful towns and beach resorts just 20–30 kilometres from Lisbon

Casino Estoril   £29
Every evening
Dinner, cabaret and casino

SURCHARGES

There are no extra surcharges. Once you have booked your holiday and paid your deposit, there are no additional costs.

CHILD REDUCTIONS

We offer children aged 2–11 a £25 reduction – as long as they share a room with two adults paying the full price.

Unit 21 NOTHING SUCCEEDS LIKE SUCCESS Exercise 3

A promising young skier had a very serious car accident and was told by doctors that she would never ski again. However, she dedicated her whole life to building up her strength, and eventually to everyone's amazement, she returned to skiing and won a medal at the Winter Olympics.

If ....

....

Unit 11 CAN YOU SELL IT? Exercise 6

ROSE-TINTED

LOOK AT LIFE IN A NEW WAY

INSTANTLY CURES DEPRESSION

FED UP? Depressed by those dull, dull days? Then get a pair of ROSE TINTED SPECTACLES and see life as politicians do

£7.99 Inc. VAT

SPECS

Buy 2 pairs get one FREE No one should be without them

TAPESCRIPTS

Full photocopiable tapescripts are in the Teacher's Book.

Tapescript 1 (Unit 13, Review and development)
1. Do people wear caps on their heads?
2. Are boots normally made of cotton?
3. Do people wear gloves on their feet?
4. Is a jumper the same as a pullover?
5. Do you wear socks over your shoes?
6. Can you keep money in a purse?
7. Are tights made of leather?
8. Is a skirt another name for a dress?
9. Can you try on clothes in a boutique?
10. If something fits you, is it the right size?
11. Are trainers edible?
12. Are jumpers usually reversible?
13. Can you have a dress shortened?
14. Do people wear suits when they play tennis?
15. Do seat belts hold up your trousers?

Tapescript 2 (Unit 15, Review and development)
1. Can you walk on a path?
2. Is there grass on a lawn?
3. Can you swim on a cliff?
4. Do sparrows have wings?
5. Is a goat a type of animal?
6. Is an eagle a type of fish?
7. Can you hop on two legs?
8. Can you creep through bushes?
9. Can a fence gallop?
10. Do helicopters land?
11. If you bump into someone, do you meet them?
12. Can motorbikes skid?
13. Can you cancel a lake?
14. Do alarm clocks go off?
15. Is grammar fun?

Tapescript 3 (Unit 18, Good news, bad news)
Good morning. This is the eight o'clock news and here are today's headlines:

Inflation falls for the third time this year.

The year long industrial dispute at the Robinson factory has ended with massive redundancies.

The first peaceful multi-party elections in Atora have brought victory to the People's party.

The drought in Zebrina is threatening to lead to famine in the coming months.

And defeat for Canada in last night's ice hockey final.

Tapescript 4 (Unit 19, Writing a curriculum vitae)
A good CV, a CV that's, that's going to work for you and get you interviews, should always be brief and to the point. You shouldn't include information that's not relevant to the job that you're applying for.

Um, sentences ought to be short and, and businesslike, and then they'll hold the reader's attention. It ought to start with your name, your address, phone number, and personal details including your age, your marital status, and then continue on with professional and educational qualifications. Previous jobs ought to be, ought to be listed in, in reverse order, that is with the, er, the most recent job at the top of the list, and then working down back to when your work life started. But again, bearing in mind that the CV has to be short – I mean, you needn't list everything. In my opinion the perfect CV shouldn't be longer than two pages. And, er, when you've finished it, er, send it out with ... you should send it out with a covering letter explaining why you think you're suitable for the job. And if you're not available for an interview at, at certain times, then you should also make that very clear in your letter. You don't want to be offered an interview and then have to say you can't make it because of some other commitment.

IRREGULAR VERBS AND PHONETIC SYMBOLS

Irregular verbs

Infinitive	Past simple	Past participle
be	was/were	been
become	became	become
begin	began	begun
bend	bent	bent
bite	bit	bitten
blow	blew	blown
break	broke	broken
bring	brought	brought
build	built	built
buy	bought	bought
can	could	(been able)
catch	caught	caught
choose	chose	chosen
come	came	come
cost	cost	cost
cut	cut	cut
do	did	done
draw	drew	drawn
dream	dreamt	dreamt
drink	drank	drunk
drive	drove	driven
eat	ate	eaten
fall	fell	fallen
feel	felt	felt
fight	fought	fought
find	found	found
fly	flew	flown
forget	forgot	forgotten
get	got	got
give	gave	given
go	went	gone (been)
have	had	had
hear	heard	heard
hit	hit	hit
hold	held	held
hurt	hurt	hurt
keep	kept	kept
know	knew	known
learn	learnt	learnt
leave	left	left
lend	lent	lent
let	let	let
lie	lay	lain
lose	lost	lost
make	made	made
mean	meant	meant
meet	met	met
pay	paid	paid
put	put	put
read /riːd/	read /red/	read /red/
ride	rode	ridden
ring	rang	rung
rise	rose	risen
run	ran	run
say	said	said
see	saw	seen
sell	sold	sold
send	sent	sent
set	set	set
shake	shook	shaken
shine	shone	shone
shoot	shot	shot
show	showed	shown
shut	shut	shut
sing	sang	sung
sit	sat	sat
sleep	slept	slept
speak	spoke	spoken
spell	spelt	spelt
spend	spent	spent
stand	stood	stood
steal	stole	stolen
swim	swam	swum
take	took	taken
teach	taught	taught
tell	told	told
think	thought	thought
throw	threw	thrown
understand	understood	understood
wake	woke	woken
wear	wore	worn
win	won	won
write	wrote	written

Phonetic symbols

Vowels

Symbol	Example
/iː/	see
/i/	happy
/ɪ/	big
/e/	bed
/æ/	sad
/ʌ/	sun
/ɑː/	car
/ɒ/	pot
/ɔː/	taught
/ʊ/	pull
/uː/	boot
/ɜː/	bird
/ə/	among
	produce
/eɪ/	date
/aɪ/	time
/ɔɪ/	boy
/əʊ/	note
/aʊ/	town
/ɪə/	ear
/eə/	there
/ʊə/	tour

Consonants

Symbol	Example
/b/	back
/d/	dog
/ð/	then
/dʒ/	joke
/f/	far
/g/	go
/h/	hot
/j/	young
/k/	key
/l/	learn
/m/	make
/n/	note
/ŋ/	sing
/p/	pan
/r/	ran
/s/	soon
/ʃ/	fish
/t/	top
/tʃ/	chart
/θ/	thin
/v/	view
/w/	went
/z/	zone
/ʒ/	pleasure

Stress

Stress is indicated by a small box above the stressed syllable.
Example: advertisement

ACKNOWLEDGEMENTS

Authors' acknowledgements
We would like to thank Stephen Slater for his original inspiration in the development of *True to Life*.

We are also very grateful to Gillian Lazar for her continued support and perceptive criticisms on the final manuscript.

Friends and colleagues have given us permission to use their ideas and activities – or in some cases given us inspiration. We would therefore like to thank Philip Dale, Clare Fletcher, Jackie Gresham, Frances Eales, Susan Barduhn, Terry Miles, Tim Shirra and Frances Gairns. As ever, a big thank you to all our colleagues at International House and The London School of English for their ideas, support and kindness.

We would also like to express our gratitude to writers whose work has influenced us in specific activities: Trisha Hedge, Jill Hadfield and Mark Bartram and Richard Walton.

At Cambridge University Press, we would like to thank James Dingle for his coordination of the pilot edition, and very sincere thanks to Kate Boyce for her excellent management of the project and unfailing support. Helena Gomm's contribution has been immense and we have much appreciated her humour; we are also most grateful to Nick Newton and Randell Harris for their impressive and stylish design and production work.

We would like to thank Martin Williamson for his considerable help and guidance on the listening material and to all the actors involved and to the staff of AVP.

Finally, our thanks go to the commissioning editor, Peter Donovan, who set the project in motion, and to the rest of the staff at Cambridge University Press.

The authors and publishers would like to thank the following institutions and teachers for their help in testing the material and for the invaluable feedback which they provided:
AVL, Paris, France; BTL, Paris, France; Diann Gruber, Paris, France; Associazone Culturale Delle Lingue Europee, Bologna, Italy; British Council, Milan, Italy; Civica Scuola di Lingue, Milan, Italy; Cambridge English Studies, La Coruña, Spain; Roger Scott, Eurocentres, Bournemouth, UK; Hampstead Garden Suburb Institute, London, UK.

The authors and publishers are grateful to the following copyright holders for permission to reproduce copyright material. While every endeavour has been made, it has not been possible to identify the sources of all material used and in such cases the publishers would welcome information from copyright sources. Apologies are expressed for any omissions.
p. 14: Longman Group for the first dictionary entry; p. 14: HarperCollins for the second dictionary entry; p. 16: HarperCollins for the first dictionary entry; p. 36: *The Independent* for the article about children 25/10/92; p. 41: Longman Group for the first dictionary entry; p. 41: HarperCollins for the second dictionary entry; *The Independent* for the article 'Have we queued our last?' 2/1/94; p. 46: Brandreth Gyles for the extract from *Gyles Brandreth's Book Of Puzzles and Brainteasers*, published by Octopus Books, reproduced by permission of Reed International Books; p. 49: *Reader's Digest* for the extract from 'Where Jeeves Learns To Serve'; p. 51: Hugh Morrison for the extract from *Acting Skills*, published and reproduced by permission of A & C Black; p. 57: 'Vroom's decision tree model' from *Understanding Organisations* by Charles Handy (Penguin Books 1976, fourth edition 1993) copyright © Charles Handy, 1976, 1981, 1985, 1993; p. 62: *New Penguin Guide To The Law* by John Pritchard (Viking 1982, third edition 1993) copyright © John Pritchard, 1982, 1986, 1993; p. 70: *The Guardian* for the extract 'Please don't call me and I won't call you' by Jim Shelley; p. 73: *Girl about Town Magazine* for the questionnaire; p. 83: Elizabeth Holt for the extract from *The Big Book of Facts, Records and Lists*, published by Piccolo Books and reproduced by permission of Pan Macmillan; p. 84: *Business Traveller Magazine* for the extract 'Kitted Out' by Caroline Fossey, © *Business Traveller Magazine*; p. 90: *Reader's Digest* for the extract from 'On Trial – Our Jury System' by Fenton Bressler; p. 96: *The Independent* for the article 'Making fun of grammar' by Sarah Lonsdale 24/10/93; pp. 103 and 172: *Reader's Digest* for the extracts from 'How To Tackle Noisy Neighbours' by Robert Kiener; p. 111: Peiffer Vera for the extract from *Positive Thinking*, published and reproduced by permission of Element Books; p. 112: John G Muir for the extract from *More Classroom Clangers*, published and reproduced by permission of Gordon Wright Publishing Limited; p. 117: Office of Fair Trading for the extract from their Holiday List; p. 118: Thompson Tour Operations Limited; p. 122: Parker Dorothy for the extract from 'A Telephone Call' taken from *The Collected Dorothy Parker*, reproduced by permission of Gerald Duckworth & Co. Ltd; p. 126: *Reader's Digest* for the extract from 'Lecture at RSA'; p. 130: Plain English Campaign for the extracts from *14th Awards Leaflet (December 1993)* and *The Crystal Mark*; p. 131: *Daily Mail* for the extract 'Hire Me, I'm a quick leaner', 10/2/94, reproduced by permission of Solo Syndications; p. 133: *New Woman Magazine* for the article 'Speak Up' by Karen

Taylor, March 1994; p. 138: *The Guardian* for the extract 'Artists at Court' 31/07/91; p. 139: *The European* for the extract 'You've seen the paintings – now buy the jewels' 21-7/01/94; p. 144: *Woman's Realm* for the article 'Sprechen Sie Deutsch?' 18/01/94, reproduced by permission of Solo Syndications; p. 147: *The Independent* for the article 'The down side of being outward bound' by Hester Lacy; p. 149: *The Observer* for the extract 'Painting by numbers' 13/2/94; p. 151: *The Independent* for the article 'We crept out into utter devastation' by Mary Williams; p. 153: *Reader's Digest* for the extracts from 'Home Remedies Even Doctors Use' by Catherine Clifford;

The authors and publishers are grateful to the following illustrators and photographic sources:
Illustrators: David Atkinson: p. 136; Gerry Ball: p. 49; Veronica Bailey: p. 47; David Barnett: p. 144; Kathy Baxendale: p. 82; Peter Byatt: pp. 15, 106; Paul Dickinson: p. 59; David Downton: pp. 89, 121; Nicky Dupays: pp. 11, 39, 85, 115, 120; Max Ellis: pp. 10, 71, 97; Philip Emms: pp. 13, 35 *t*, 45, 107; Annie Farrall: pp. 23, 84; Martin Fish: pp. 42, 88, 131; Spike Gerrell: p. 129; Michael Hill: pp. 16 *b*, 78; Sue Hillwood-Harris: p. 95; Terry Kennett: pp. 50, 119; Joanna Kerr: pp. 66, 92, 114; Edward McLachlan: p. 100; Cathy Morley: p. 26; Diane Oliver: pp. 9, 68, 108, 110, 127, 141; Mark Peppé: pp. 122, 123; Giovanna Pierce: pp. 32, 80, 154; Tracy Rich: pp. 19, 34, 35 *b*, 81, 103; Sunita Singh: pp. 57, 94; Sue Smickler: pp. 53, 93; Judy Stevens: pp. 76, 156; Jane Strother: p. 150; Phillip Tyler: p. 37; Annabel Wright: pp. 16 *t*, 74, 83.
Photographic sources: Ace Photo Agency: pp. 25 (luggage photo Mauritius), 25 (writing paper photo Jackson), 40 (Searle, two photos), 46 *br* (Panton), 58 *r* (Palmer), 62 *tc* (Begg), 62 *b* (Sims), 77 no. 8 (T and J Florian), 86 *br* (Burns), 104 *tr* (Mauritius) and 110 *c* (Searle); Allsport UK: p. 147 *b* (Vandystadt); BBC Photo Library: p. 22 *l* and *r*; John Birdsall Photography: pp. 40 no. 10, 60 (old age), 86 *tc* and *tr*; Britstock IFA: pp. 21 *tc* (Bach), 21 *bc* (Selma), 25 (antique clock photo Zscharnack), 40 no. 9 (Fred) and 60 (child photo Gunther); Bubbles Photo Library: pp. 6 *cr* (West) and 60 (child photo Price); Camera Press: pp. 7 *cl* (P. J. Couderc), 7 *tr* (Pasan/RBO), 7 *br* (Ridgers), 40 nos. 3 and 5 (Hancer), 125 *tl* (B/S Port) and 125 *br* (Ajansi); Carlton UK Television: p. 22 *cl* and *cr*; Collections: p. 40 no. 8 (Sieveking); Colorific: p. 132 *c* (Bradshaw); Zoe Dominic: p. 105; Greg Evans International: pp. 62 *t*, 64 *t*, 117 (3 photos) and 118 (3 photos); Garden Picture Library: p. 52 *t* (Lamontage); Ronald Grant Archive: pp. 50 *r* and 90 *t* and *cl*; *The Guardian*: p. 138, the photograph 'Artists at Court' (Gary Weasser); Robert Harding Picture Library: pp. 6 *cl* (Hughes), 25 (toy and kite clock), 60 (adult *1* photo Westlight), 64 *b*, 110 *l* (Explorer), 147 *t* (Francis) and 173 (Tomlinson); Houses and Interiors: p. 25 (dining table); Hulton Deutsch Collection: p. 34 *tr* and *b*; Hutchison Library: pp. 6 *t* (Simcock), 21 *t* (Hunter), 21 *b* (Stock-photo/Wilkinson), 40 no. 6 (de Lossy), 40 no. 12 (Berwin), 46 *tl* (Dee), 46 *tr* (Hart), 54 *r* (de Lossy), 56 *b* (Miller), 104 *tl* (Hamilton) and 132 *r* (Klumpp); David King Collection: p. 116 *tl*; Moviestore Collection: pp. 34 *tl*, 50 *l*, *cl*, *cr* and 90 *cl*; Vera Peiffer: p. 111; Photo Researchers, New York: p. 90 *b*; Powerstock Photo Library: pp. 56 *c*, 60 (adult *r* photo Nelson) and 132 *l*; Range Pictures: p. 122 (Bettman); Retna Pictures: pp. 7 *cr* (Acheson), 69 *t* (Acheson), 104 *br* (Wood) and 116 *tr*; Réunion des Musées Nationaux, Paris: p. 139 *tl* Alfred Stevens, *Le Bain*, *tr* Degas, *Au Café dit L'Absinthe*, and *br* Cézanne, *Le Vase Bleu*; Rex Features: pp. 7 *tl*, 25 (wig and tennis), 40 no. 7 (Kaiser), 40 no. 11 (Today), 124 *bc* (Sipa), 124 *r* (Brutmann), 125 *tc* (Sipa), 125 *tr* (Today) and 151; Royal Shakespeare Company: p. 51 (John Haynes); Peter Sanders: p. 63 *t*; Simpson Fox Associates: p. 126; Tony Stone Worldwide: pp. 43 *r* (Johnson), 54 *l* (Bosler) and 145 (Bramley); Swedish Travel and Tourism Council: p. 82; Tate Gallery: p. 149 *Light Red Over Black*, 1957, by Mark Rothko © ARS, NY and DACS, London 1996; Telegraph Colour Library: pp. 6 *b* (VCL), 60 (adolescent photo FPG/Tilley); Topham Picturepoint: pp. 7 *bl*, 43 *l*, 43 *c* (UBB), 63 *b*, 86 *bl* and 110 *r*.

The photos on pp. 12, 14, 20, 29, 40 (nos. 1 and 4), 58 *l*, 75, 77 (except no. 8), 87, 95, 134, 137, 143, 146 and 153 were taken by Trevor Clifford.

We would also like to thank *Newsweek, Reader's Digest, Cosmopolitan, Hello!, Paris Match, ¡Hola!, National Geographic* and *Marie Claire* magazines for permission to photograph the front covers on pp. 28 and 30.

t = top, *b* = bottom, *c* = centre, *l* = left, *r* = right

Design and DTP by Newton Harris
Picture research by Marilyn Rawlings

The authors are publishers are grateful to the following for permission to reproduce photographs on the cover:
Comstock Photo Library, forest; Image Bank, eyes by David de Lossy, Marc Grimberg, Juan Alvarez and Nancy Brown; Newton Harris, background left; Pictor International, two photos of eyes; Tony Stone Worldwide, island by Pascal Crapet, eyes by Bruce Ayres (two photos), James Darell and Gerrard Loucel.